STUDIES IN AMERICAN LITERATURE

Volume XV

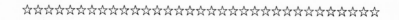

THE
COLUMBIAN MAGAZINE
AND AMERICAN
LITERARY NATIONALISM

by

WILLIAM J. FREE

1968

MOUTON

THE HAGUE · PARIS

For Ruby Ann and David

PREFACE

The early national period of American literature extended from the end of the Revolution to the eighteen-twenties at which time William Cullen Bryant, James Fenimore Cooper, and Washington Irving became the first American authors to achieve international reputations. The period was one of contradiction, confusion, and experimentation as American culture attempted to break away from its colonial antecedents and establish its unique national identity. But a literature breaks away from the continuity of its tradition at its own risk, and American writers found the silver cord difficult to cut. For four decades after the end of the Revolution, the form, content, and themes of eighteenth-century English literature and the urge for Americanism in letters existed in an unstable tension. English forms and content were tortured into confessing American ideals; American content was forced into English forms and made to express the universal ideas of neo-classicism. Only after writers learned to adjust their national aspirations to their linguistic and literary heritage did American literature become free to forge its own identity.

The purpose of this study is to document from the pages of one prominent magazine of the period the pressures that shaped early American literary nationalism. The ingredients are familiar to students of English and American literature; the particular mixture is significant because it throws light on the struggle to achieve national literary expression and the resolution of that struggle. Although it published little of lasting aesthetic merit, the *Columbian Magazine* illuminates the context from which the literature of the American Renaissance emerged.

Professor George F. Horner of the University of North Carolina gave invaluable guidance to the first version of this study, and I am deeply indebted to him for many reasons. I would like also to thank Deans Gerald Huff of the Graduate School and Robert A. McRorie, Director of General Research, of the University of Georgia, who have generously made time and funds available to aid in the completion of this study.

TABLE OF CONTENTS

1

THE STRUGGLE FOR A NATIONAL MAGAZINE

In a sense, American literature did not begin until after the Revolution. During the colonial period Americans looked to London as the center of their cultural life. The colonial cultural heritage was English, and at first Americans quarreled with the Crown over the rights of free-born Englishmen, not for independence and nationality. Even when the Second Continental Congress met in May 1775 there was little nationalistic sentiment. But the surrender of Cornwallis at Yorktown on October 19, 1781, effected more than the cessation of hostilities; it left Americans with an intense sense of their national identity. Tom Paine had written in "The Crisis": "It is not every country (perhaps there is not another in the world) that can boast so fair an origin"; and Americans were quick to transfer their political uniqueness to culture. Flushed with victory, they demanded, not only in government but in every phase of life – language, education, manners, fashion, art, and even whiskey and cosmetics [1] – principles and mores demonstrably compatible with the ideology of republicanism.

Those concerned with the nation's letters sought a native

---

[1] *The Columbian Magazine; or, Monthly Miscellany* (November 1788), p. 628 asserts that American cornstarch is the finest cosmetic in the world, and *ibid.* (November 1790), 325 proposes a "truly FEDERAL wine". For purposes of consistency, I will, throughout this book, refer to the magazine as the *Columbian Magazine*, although the official title changed in March 1790 to *The Universal Asylum and Columbian Magazine*. All subsequent references to the magazine will appear in the text and will include month, year, and pagination. Volume numbers will not be used since they changed bi-annually and are ambiguous of the change of title.

American literature comparable in quality to that of ancient Greece and Rome; and, with an innocent faith in the efficacy of democracy to accomplish all Utopias, they set out to realize that achievement. Although their optimism blinded them to the difficulties of the task (difficulties of which the literary generation from 1815 to 1850 was more painfully aware), their early struggles to realize classical greatness in American literature is important because, as Leon Howard has pointed out, "The achievement of American literature in the early nineteenth century was that of reconciling some of the conflicts that had arisen in the period before, and a genuine understanding of this achievement may be reached, perhaps, only through a recognition of some of the problems revealed in the less intrinsically interesting literature of the earlier 'age of contradictions'." [2]

The medium through which Americans hoped to stimulate national culture was the magazine. Twenty-seven new magazines began publication from 1775 to 1795, six more than in all the previous history of American periodicals. They reveal, more clearly than any other medium, the literary currents and tastes of the time.

Most of these magazines were dedicated to cultural nationalism. Their editors and publishers reasoned that, since European literature had achieved complete development in the eighteenth century and was thereafter destined to repeat itself, only America offered the new images and new ideas that would insure the continued improvement of art. They agreed with David Ramsay, who wrote in the *United States Magazine* in 1779: "Ever since the flood, true religion, literature, arts, empire, and riches, have taken a slow and gradual course from east to west, and are now about fixing their long and favourite abode in this new western world."

Most American men of letters in the 1780's believed that national literary greatness was imminent. Timothy Dwight expressed the belief that "in our happy state of society, disjointed from the customs and systems of Europe, it is to be ardently

[2] "The Late Eighteenth Century", *Transitions in American Literary History*, ed. Harry Hayden Clark (Durham, N. C., Duke University Press, 1954), 89.

hoped, that so much independence of mind will be assumed by us, as to induce us to shake off those rusty shackels" of European domination, and, viewing nature with clear-headed republican simplicity, produce a great literature.[3] The *Royal American Magazine* extended national loyalty even to the materials with which it was printed, a policy which forced the printer to apologize that "The INK also has been poor, but as it was of AMERICAN MANUFACTURE my customers were not only willing but desirous that I should use it".[4] One anonymous writer in the *New Haven Gazette and Connecticut Magazine* in May 1786 optimistically asserted that American literature was already as great as English and that John Trumbull possessed poetical genius equal to Swift's. Many other comparable statements appeared in American magazines in the years immediately following the Revolution. Americans were launched on a great experiment in national letters and were to remain self-consciously aware of their destiny for decades to come.[5]

Amid this spirit of literary chauvinism, five Philadelphians, Mathew Carey, William Spotswood, James Trenchard, Charles Cist, and Thomas Seddon, banded together during the late summer of 1786 to create a new periodical, *The Columbian*

---

[3]   "The Friend", No. IV. Quoted in Clarence Arthur Brown, *The Achievement of American Criticism* (New York, Ronald Press, 1954), 62-65.

[4]   Quoted in Frank Luther Mott, *A History of American Magazines* (Cambridge, Mass., The Belknap Press of Harvard University Press, 1957), I, 86. All my comments on the history of American magazines are, of course, heavily indebted to Mott's definitive study and to Lyon Richardson, *A History of Early American Magazines* (New York, Thomas Nelson and Sons, 1931).

[5]   The standard study of American literary nationalism is Benjamin T. Spencer, *The Quest for Nationality* (Syracuse, N. Y., Syracuse University Press, 1957). An informative and detailed unpublished study is Charles W. Cole, "Beginnings of Literary Nationalism 1775-1800", Ph.D. dissertation, Department of English, George Washington University, 1939. In addition to these two studies, my comments on literary nationalism are indebted to Merle Curti, *The Growth of American Thought* (New York, 1943); Merrill Jensen, *The New Nation: A History of the United States During the Confederation 1781-1789* (New York, 1950); Howard Mumford Jones, *O Strange New World* (New York, 1964); Hans Kohn, *American Nationalism* (New York, 1957); and Russel Blaine Nye, *The Cultural Life of the New Nation* (New York, 1960).

Magazine; or, Monthly Miscellany. Like the publishers of all eighteenth-century American magazines they modeled their efforts on the most popular of English miscellany magazines, Cave's *Gentleman's Magazine.* They promised to print "as great a variety of original essays, instructive and entertaining, as the extent of the work will admit . . ." in a forty-eight page format "elegantly printed on a very neat paper, of American manufacture". The *Columbian* would appear on the first day of every month beginning October 1, 1786, would include two copperplate engravings in each issue, and would cost twenty shillings a year or twenty-five cents a single copy. The publishers insisted on the high seriousness of their undertaking and assured their potential subscribers that:

> This design has been taken up after mature deliberation: we shall not, therefore, rashly abandon it. We are fully determined to conduct the undertaking, as to merit the public attention; for which purpose every exertion shall be made, on our parts: – and the generous support of which we have been assured, added to the high estimation we have conceived of the taste, liberality and patriotic spirit of our respectable fellow citizens, justify our confidence of success.[6]

The first issue appeared on October 4, 1786, four days late.

The *Columbian* was the most important American magazine published in the eighteenth century for several reasons. First, when it died in December 1792, it had accomplished a longer run than any previous American magazine, six years and four months. Of all eighteenth-century American magazines, only the *Massachusetts Magazine* and the *New York Magazine* completed longer runs, and both began four years after the *Columbian.* The *Columbian* was the first American miscellany magazine to accomplish a run of over three years and the first post-Revolutionary magazine to achieve stable continuity.

Secondly, the *Columbian* had the largest circulation of any eighteenth-century American magazine. Only when Joseph

---

[6] Quoted from an advertisement announcing the beginning of the *Columbian Magazine* in the *Pennsylvania Packet* (Friday, September 1, 1786). The same advertisement appeared twice weekly in the *Packet* and other Philadelphia papers during the month of September.

Dennie's *Port Folio* reached a circulation of 2,000 in 1801 was the *Columbian* surpassed; and even as late as 1820 the respected *North American Magazine* could count only 600 subscribers, less than half the number the *Columbian* had reached thirty years earlier.

Thirdly, the *Columbian* vigorously sought the best original American material available. It was the first magazine to pay contributors and to solicit material regularly from the public. In contrast, its chief rival the *American Museum* made no attempt to print original material for the first four years of its life; the *Massachusetts Magazine*, as its life extended, depended increasingly upon excerpts from foreign publications, and the *New York Magazine* clipped most of its material from other sources. Only Noah Webster's short-lived *American Magazine*, which he admitted was modeled on the *Columbian*,[7] attempted to use as much original material.

But, most important, the *Columbian* explicitly dedicated itself to the promotion of the ideal of a national literature. In the prospectus to the publication, the publishers announced that:

At the present aera, when the genuine spirit of liberty has extended its benign influence over these independent and highly favoured republics – when the encouragement of literature, the natural concomitant of FREEDOM, engages the attention of a great majority of those entrusted with power, or possessed of influence, throughout the union, the subscribers are induced respectfully, to solicit the patronage of the free citizens of the North-America. . . .

In the preface to the first issue, they reiterated their determination to "be regarded as a contemporary evidence of the progress of literature and the arts among [American] citizens. . . ." These two statements epitomize the demand for a distinctively national culture. Most American writers of the time believed that political freedom had opened the gates of a new Eden and that America's literary achievement would shout to the world her greatness. In everyone's mind freedom meant perfection, and the proprietors

---

[7] Noah Webster to William Young, New York, August 2, 1788, Dreer Manuscript Collection of American Prose Writers, Vol. 9, Historical Society of Pennsylvania, Philadelphia.

of the *Columbian* began their adventure optimistically, convinced that a golden age of letters would inevitably follow the achievement of national identity.

The editors attempted to embody this nationalistic ideal in the magazine's format. Wherever possible they began each issue with an article of strong national appeal. Each of the first two issues opened with Mathew Carey's biography of Revolutionary hero General Nathaniel Greene. In November 1786 the editors appealed to the growing interest in the antiquity of the American Indian by opening the issue with a "Description of Bones, etc. found near the River Ohio". In January and February 1787 David Humphreys' controversial "Letters relative to the treatment of Captain Asgill, while prisoner in the American army; being a full refutation of the charges of inhumanity exhibited in London against General Washington", a piece which capitalized on public interest in a scandal surrounding the national hero, appeared as the lead article. Over a period of years the magazine used biographies of such famous Americans as John Winthrop, Captain John Smith, Benjamin Franklin, and Francis Hopkinson; descriptions of the American landscape; articles on American manners; and, for eight months in 1789, a history of the Revolution to begin each issue with writings of national appeal. In addition, the magazine concluded with two features motivated by the national spirit. One was the "Columbian Parnassiad", a selection of American poetry which provides an accurate sampling of the types and quality of verse being written and admired in late eighteenth-century America. The other was the "Intelligence", which excerpted news from papers in a number of American cities. With contributions such as these, which represented the best American writing of their time and consciously appealed to patriotic spirits, the proprietors believed that they could establish a successful magazine that would be a cultural ornament to the nation.

But their sanguine expectations were never realized. Income lagged behind expenditures during the entire run of the magazine. Original contributions proved scarce. The history of the venture traveled a path of disappointed hopes and frustrated ambitions.

The management was notoriously unstable: the original owners reneged after six months, the first editor after four. Only the force of the national ideal kept the magazine alive for six and a half years.

Had profit alone spurred the owners, the *Columbian* would probably have failed after a few months as did so many of its contemporaries. But the owners accepted the eschewal of profit as concomitant with their mission to further the intellectual and cultural life of the nation, and they continued in spite of loss. In their "Address to the Public" in 1789, they informed their patrons that the expenses of the magazine had been so heavy that it was "by no means a source of emolument . . .", reminded their readers that all previous American magazines had been discontinued because of financial failure, and confessed that "had the proprietors of *this* work been actuated by motives of profit alone, *it* might also have been discontinued" (January 1789, p. ii). But, they continued, their sense of obligation to the nation forced them to continue the magazine in an era "rendered illustrious, by one of the most glorious and important events in the history of mankind". Only such a missionary zeal can explain their determination to succeed with an endeavor which all odds doomed to failure.

I

Had experienced management alone sufficed to insure success, the future of the *Columbian* would have been bright. The original owners possessed all the talents necessary to run a magazine. Mathew Carey brought to the venture eleven years' experience as a printer, bookseller, author, and editor. After several years working on other papers, he began his first periodical, the *Volunteer's Journal*, in his native Dublin, Ireland, in 1783. But, because, as his biographer has stated, "self-interest and a propitiatory attitude towards officialdom were never at any time strong features of his character . . .",[8] he was forced into exile in

8   Earl L. Bradsher, *Mathew Carey* (New York, 1912), 2.

Philadelphia where, with $400 borrowed from the Marquis de Lafayette and a letter of recommendation from Benjamin Franklin, he began the *Pennsylvania Evening Herald* in January 1785. There can be no doubt that Carey initiated the *Columbian*. He was an ambitious printer and a zealous republican who used every opportunity to increase his influence and enlarge his publishing empire. Creating a national periodical like the *Columbian* would have satisfied his desire to play an active role in promoting the new national culture.

We know little of William Spotswood except that he, too, was a recent immigrant (perhaps he had come over with Carey) and that he was a partner with Carey and Christopher Talbot in a printing business. In 1785 Spotswood had begun editing the *Complete Counting House Companion,* a free supplement to Carey's *Pennsylvania Evening Herald,* and during the first year of the *Columbian's* life he was briefly owner and editor of the *Herald.* Although an experienced journalist, Spotswood was a poor businessman; he failed in all of his ventures and moved to Boston sometime between 1790 and 1795.[9]

Of the original proprietors of the *Columbian,* the almost unknown Charles Cist had perhaps the most interesting career, the most valuable experience, and the largest financial resources. Born Charles Jacob Sigismund Thiel, Jr., on August 15, 1738, in Petersburg, Russia, Cist studied medicine at the University of Halle and was attached to the court of Catherine the Great as physician and pharmacist. When some unknown political intrigue forced him to flee Russia, he emigrated to Pennsylvania and disguised his identity by creating a new name from the initials of his Russian name. Unable to practice medicine, he apprenticed himself to Germantown printer John Heinrich Miller and in 1775 opened a job press at the corner of Roat's Alley and Second Street in Philadelphia in partnership with a German named Melchior Steiner. In 1776 the partners printed Tom Paine's *American Crisis* and the first translation of the Declaration of

---

[9]   The last record of Spotswood is as a stationer and bookseller at 55 Marlborough Street, Boston, in December 1800. A catalogue of his wares is listed in Evans, *American Bibliography,* item 37012.

Independence into a foreign language, German. The British destroyed their press in 1777; but after the occupation they purchased the press of their mentor John Heinrich Miller and continued to print his profitable German-language newspaper *Der Wochentliche Philadelphische Staatesbote*. By 1781 Cist had amassed considerable wealth; in 1784 he purchased the Philadelphia *American Herald*. His wide experience as a publisher, his ability as a translator, and his wealth made him a valuable partner in a venture such as the *Columbian*.[10]

The other two partners, James Trenchard and Thomas Seddon, left little record of their activities. Trenchard, the son of a pre-Revolutionary attorney general of New Jersey, was working in Philadelphia as an engraver and seal cutter in June 1777. Evidence of his work survives in a few portraits, his copperplates for the *Columbian*, and a medal cast for the Agricultural Society of Philadelphia in 1790. In June 1789 Ebenezer Hazard wrote Jeremy Belknap that Trenchard was thinking of moving to Boston because of family troubles, but the exact nature of the trouble was never clarified.[11] In other letters Trenchard appears to be a man unsure of himself and tormented by fears of failure. David McNeeley Stauffer believes that he went to England in 1793 and remained there.[12]

Thomas Seddon is known only as the proprietor of a large stationery and book shop in Philadelphia and as subscription agent for the *Columbian* throughout its life.

Had this talented group of proprietors retained control of the

[10] In 1792 Cist was one of the originators of the Lehigh Coal Mine Company and in 1800 he was appointed public printer for the federal government during the John Adams administration. See John Clyde Oswold, *Printing in the Americas* (New York, 1937), 153-154; John Joseph Stoudt, "The German Press in Philadelphia and the American Revolution", *Pennsylvania Magazine of History and Biography*, LIX (1935), 74-98; and Townsend Ward, "North Second Street and its Associations", *Pennsylvania Magazine of History and Biography*, IV (1880), 42-60.

[11] "Belknap Papers", *Collections of the Massachusetts Historical Society*, 5th Ser. (Boston, 1877), III, 146. Much of our knowledge of the history of the *Columbian Magazine* comes from the correspondence of Jeremy Belknap. All records and papers of the magazine have disappeared.

[12] *American Engravers upon Steel and Copper* (New York, 1907), I, 276.

magazine for a consequential period of time, its history might have been even more distinguished. But the motivating force behind the magazine, Mathew Carey, withdrew from the proprietorship in February 1787. Perhaps, as Frank Luther Mott has suggested, he found "too many fingers in the pie" when working with four partners; [13] or, as Lyon Richardson speculates, he may have been dissatisfied with the prospects of the *Columbian* and desired to publish a magazine of his own.[14] At any rate, in mid-November 1786 he began taking subscriptions for his new *American Museum*, the first issue of which appeared on February 1, 1787; and on February 10 the firm of Carey, Talbot and Spotswood announced that it was dissolving "by mutual consent".[15]

After Carey's withdrawal, the magazine entered a period of relative stability which saw the partnership become increasingly dominated by William Spotswood. Spotswood continued to print the magazine after the dissolving of his partnership with Carey, and, by September 1787, he spoke with the voice of authority on the question of hiring a new editor. At the end of 1787 he became sole proprietor when his partners Cist, Trenchard, and Seddon withdrew for financial reasons. During all of 1788 he was in complete control of the magazine.

But, as the fall of 1788 lengthened, Spotswood found continuing the magazine increasingly difficult. His letters during October and November gave a dismal account of his prospects. He reported that circulation was declining in Pennsylvania and that "the payments I have monthly to make are heavy, and must be answered, which are paper, copperplate engraving, the editor, etc., the weight of which I begin now sensibly to feel, and with difficulty can continue to answer them".[16]

---

13 *History of American Magazines*, I, 100.
14 *Early American Magazines*, 278.
15 Their announcement appeared in the *Pennsylvania Herald* for January 13, 1787. Proof that Carey was taking subscriptions for the *Museum* as early as mid-November can be found in a letter from William Harrison to Mathew Carey, Charleston, November 10, 1786, Mathew Carey Papers, Historical Society of Pennsylvania, Philadelphia.
16 "Belknap Papers", 6th Ser. (1891), IV, 421.

The extent of the pinch which Spotswood was feeling can be calculated on the basis of our knowledge of the circulation and operating expenses of the magazine. The average monthly circulation throughout its life seems to have been about 1,500 copies, a figure which Spotswood specifically mentioned in a letter to Jeremy Belknap in April 1787 and which a subsequent proprietor William Young quoted in February 1792.[17] In the preface to Volume I in September 1786 the publishers said that the monthly expense of the magazine was 100 pounds. The addition of a paid editor in the spring of 1787 at the expense of 150 pounds a year, and the payment of certain contributors at the rate of a guinea per three pages of printed text raised that cost to perhaps 125 to 150 pounds a month. Thus, the twelve monthly issues plus the yearly supplement cost an estimated 1,625 to 1,950 pounds annually. If the magazine sold 1,500 copies at one pound a year, the average annual loss would have been between 125 and 450 pounds. This estimate is supported by Spotswood's statement to Belknap in October 1788 that he was forced to invest an additional 100 pounds every six months in order to meet expenses.[18] Such a loss was more than any publisher could be expected to sustain.

The inroads of new magazines and the business tactics of his former partner Mathew Carey aggravated Spotswood's financial troubles. The appearance of Isaiah Thomas's *Massachusetts Magazine* cut so deeply into Spotswood's large Boston circulation that by December 13, 1788, New England subscription agent Jeremy Belknap predicted, "I do not expect that the proprietors of the Columbian will think it worth their while to send any here after this year is out." [19] Spotswood also complained of the competition of Carey's *Museum* in Philadelphia and of Noah Webster's *American Magazine* in New York.

Carey's attempt to undersell him in New England further increased Spotswood's troubles. The standard price abatement given by magazine publishers to the booksellers who were their agents

17 *Ibid.*, 5th Ser., III, 286 and 6th Ser., IV, 331.
18 *Ibid.*, 6th Ser., IV, 421.
19 *Ibid.*, 5th Ser., III, 83.

was one-sixth of retail. But in October 1788 Carey began giving Boston booksellers a one-third abatement for handling his *Museum*, a practice which Spotswood feared would set a dangerous precedent and wreck the magazine business. He was forced to reciprocate in Boston and give an additional ten to fifteen percent for those magazines carried to rural New England, although it meant a further loss of profit. The alternative would have been to surrender his large New England circulation.[20]

Spotswood also ran into political trouble. In the winter of 1787-1788, Alexander James Dallas, who was editing both the *Columbian* and the *Pennsylvania Evening Herald* for Spotswood, angered the Federalist faction with his reporting of the debates of the Pennsylvania ratifying convention. Federalist leader Benjamin Rush branded Dallas's reporting as misrepresentation, and in response, the Federalists canceled their subscriptions to both the *Herald* and the *Columbian*.[21] Their action forced the *Herald* out of business in February 1788 and caused Spotswood considerable added financial difficulty. He afterward voiced despair about publication in Philadelphia, where

indeed, to meddle with politicks at all seemed ... likely to precipitate an unfortunate fate ... particularly in Pennsylvania, where parties carry their political opinions to a degree bordering on ill nature, if not worse. ... My study was to have steered an impartial line. This I found impracticable in Philadelphia, as the existence of a newspaper in Philadelphia depends solely on the printer's avowing himself and his paper devoted to some party. ...[22]

Plagued by politicians and shrinking financial resources, Spotswood gave up. In January 1789 he sold the *Columbian* to his former partner James Trenchard. Trenchard's hopes of success were not sanguine. Although he promised his readers that "no pains, no cost will be spared to render the *Columbian Magazine*

---

[20] *Ibid.*, 6th Ser., IV, 422-423 and 392.
[21] For Rush's comment see *Letters of Benjamin Rush*, ed. L. H. Butterfield (Princeton, 1951), I, 450. The Federalists' cancelling of their subscriptions is discussed in *Pennsylvania and the Federal Convention 1787-1788*, ed. John B. McMasters and Frederick D. Stone (Philadelphia, 1888), 15.
[22] "Belknap Papers", 6th Ser., IV, 409-410.

the most elegant, entertaining and valuable repository of the kind
that has ever appeared in America ...", he candidly admitted to
the public that if the magazine did fail to live up to expectation,
"it is hoped, that the difficulties and expense, attending an undertaking of this nature, will be admitted as an apology for its
defects" (January 1789, p. ii). Trenchard's fears were not disappointed. Circulation did not improve in spite of his efforts. In
March Trenchard visited New York, hoping to bolster circulation
there, and reported some success; but any gains were temporary.
By July there were rumors that "the dissolution of the Columbian
Magazine was approaching. ..." In October Jeremy Belknap
reported that he had lost 20 subscriptions because of the continued
growth of Thomas's *Massachusetts Magazine*.[23] Such losses, added
to the fact that Trenchard failed to increase circulation in other
areas, forced him to relinquish control of the magazine. On the
title page of the December 1789 issue, William Spotswood again
appeared as publisher.

Spotswood resumed the publication with a mood of impending
doom. He offered Jeremy Belknap a quarter interest in the venture, but at the same time advised him that a partnership was not
worth the money.[24] Although he promised the public in the
January 1790 issue that they "will have no cause of dissatisfaction
... in the future progress of the work ..." the quality of the
publication declined noticeably. All attempts to print original
subject matter ceased, and the magazine became a pastiche of
anecdotes, excerpts from foreign publications, short fiction, and
miscellaneous prose clipped from other magazines. After three
issues Spotswood gave up again.

The March 1790 issue announced a sweeping change of
publisher, printer, editor, and even title. The refurbished magazine, now entitled "*The Universal Asylum*, and *Columbian Magazine*" published by "a SOCIETY OF GENTLEMEN", opened its

---

[23] See letter of Ebenezer Hazard to Mathew Carey, Philadelphia, March
31, 1789, Mathew Carey Papers, Historical Society of Pennsylvania, Philadelphia, and "Belknap Papers", 5th Ser., III, 149 and 198 for the accounts
of Trenchard's difficulties.
[24] "Belknap Papers", 5th Ser., III, 105.

March issue with an address to "THE PATRONS OF AMERICAN LITERATURE", informing them that:

the *Columbian Magazine* had been lately transferred to *new proprietors*, between whom and the gentlemen, who sometime ago published proposals for the *Philadelphia Magazine and Universal Asylum*, an agreement, to unite the two, has taken place. The *joint-proprietors*, have, therefore, resolved to continue the Columbian Magazine, on an enlarged and improved plan. . . .

Revived by this transfusion of talent and money, the magazine continued a healthy life until December 1792, giving it the longest run of any American magazine to that date.

The identities of the "Society of Gentlemen" who had been advertising for subscriptions to the *Philadelphia Magazine and Universal Asylum* have remained unknown. Frank Luther Mott speculates that Benjamin Rush may have been one of them,[25] a guess which seems logical in the light of other evidence. Rush had long been a paid contributor to the *Columbian* and he continued to contribute to the newly remodeled magazine his own work and that of other prominent Americans like his friend Thomas Paine. Moreover, he was a cousin of James Irvine, who was probably another member of the "Society of Gentlemen". Rush's connection with the magazine during this period was well known, and it is likely that he was a partner in the new firm.

Two other members of the Society can definitely be identified: the magazine's printer William Young and General James Irvine. George Mease, in a book written less than twenty years after the *Columbian* failed, stated that Spotswood sold his interest in the magazine to Young in 1790.[26] Young was at the time a journeyman printer who had been in Spotswood's employ for some time, perhaps from the beginning of the *Columbian's* life. As owner of the *Columbian*, a magazine with an established circulation, Young was probably the principal partner in the merger with the *Philadelphia Magazine* group. He was apparently not only printer but circulation manager and general editor of the magazine from

[25] *History of American Magazines*, I, 98.
[26] *The Picture of Philadelphia* (Philadelphia, 1811), 85.

March 1790 to the end of its life. All existing correspondence concerning subscriptions is addressed to Young; and, when the magazine ceased publication in December 1792, a notice in the last issue asked creditors to call on Young to settle accounts. The wording of a letter written in January 1791 by contributor Oliver Evans of Wilmington, Delaware, to Young requesting a number of changes to be made in the text of an article he was contributing to the January issue suggests that Young also possessed editorial powers. In December 1790 Belknap spoke of Young as the man in charge of the magazine, and Young often asked Belknap for material during the period.[27] The evidence suggests that Young actually ran the magazine and that the other members of the "Society of Gentlemen" supplied financial resources and perhaps copy.

The only other member of the Society who can be identified is General James Irvine. On May 7, 1790, Belknap wrote Hazard that "I have had an application from a Mr. Irvine of Philadelphia, to engage with the proprietors of the *Asylum*"; but he did not identify which of the many Philadelphia Irvines he meant. However, a handwritten bill now in the Manuscript Collection of the Library Company of Philadelphia indicates that the man in question was General James Irvine, who had a distinguished career as a military officer, Vice President of the Supreme Executive Council of Pennsylvania, and Surveyor of Military Lands for the new federal government. In his capacity as surveyor, Irvine delivered letters and books for William Young and probably acted as subscription agent for the magazine over a wide area of the eastern seaboard and western frontier.[28]

Bertha Monica Stearns has suggested that Charles Brockden

[27] "Belknap Papers", 5th Ser., III, 240. The letter from Evans to Young is in the Autograph Manuscript Collection of the Historical Society of Pennsylvania, Philadelphia. Spotswood said that Young had "been a considerable time in my employment". "Belknap Papers", 6th Ser., IV, 420.

[28] "Belknap Papers", 5th Ser., III, 220. The bill in question is dated December 31, 1791, and is addressed from Gen. Irvine to Charles Cist for Vol. V of the *Columbian*. Evidence that Irvine carried books for Young can be found in a letter from Charles Nisbet to William Young, Carlisle, Pennsylvania, October 21, 1791, in the Manuscript Collection of the Library Company of Philadelphia.

Brown was a member of the "Society of Gentlemen", arguing that his literary activities for the Society could have given him the experience necessary for his later periodical ventures. She has even implied that perhaps the Society and Brown's Belles Lettres Club were identical; but my research found no proof of connections between the two groups. Other than Brown's "Rhapsodist" essays, no identified publication in the *Columbian* was written by a known member of the Belles Lettres Club; and, positive evidence lacking, any speculation concerning Brown's connection with the society must remain suspect.[29]

Under its new ownership and title, the *Columbian* maintained a vigorous life until the passage of the Postal Act of 1792, a bill which killed many American magazines. The Act set a fixed postal rate for newspapers and prohibited the carrying of monthly publications on any other than the maximum rate for letters and packages. Although it had previously been illegal to send periodicals through the mail, private deals with postmasters and stagecoach lines had made the distribution of magazines relatively inexpensive. But the setting of definite postage rates burdened the publishers with an added expense they could not afford. The *Columbian* editors protested in the December 1792 issue, stating that even in England and Scotland magazines were given equal postage rights with newspapers:

That this ancient and inestimable privilege of American citizens, derived to them from their British ancestors, should be wrested from them, so soon after their struggle for *equal* rights, by the very men whom they had appointed to watch over the liberties and welfare of their country, is at once a subject of astonishment and regret. – of *Astonishment*, that a legislature, in a country calling itself *republican*, should arbitrarily abridge a people of a right, which is not only enjoyed by the domestic subjects of a European *monarchy*, but is also extended to Nova-Scotia, and other foreign dependencies of that monarchy – and of *regret*, that we should so soon lose sight of those republican principles, on which the American revolution was founded,

[29]   Bertha Monica Stearns, "A Speculation Concerning Charles Brockden Brown", *Pennsylvania Magazine of History and Biography*, LIX (1935), 101 ff. The most complete treatment of Brown and the Belles Lettres Club is in David Lee Clark, *Charles Brockden Brown* (Durham, N. C., 1952), 42-49.

as to adopt a measure calculated to destroy the means of political information, and to involve the people in *more than monarchial ignorance.* . . .

But their emotional appeal to republican principles made no impact on Congress; the law stood, and the December issue was the *Columbian's* last. The expense of publishing such a journal in the United States had finally overcome the most zealous motives of nationalism.

II

In addition to financial hardship, the successive owners of the *Columbian* faced the crucial problem of finding editors. The tone, format, and quality of an early American magazine depended almost entirely on the character of its editor. Literary history, in most instances, has identified the magazine by its editor's name – Carey's *Museum*, Thomas's *Massachusetts Magazine*, Webster's *American Magazine*, Dennie's *Port Folio.* But the *Columbian* was never so fortunate as to find a strong, domineering editor whose personality shaped the publication. Editorial responsibility revolved even more often than ownership, and the quality of the individual editors fluctuated from incompetence to excellence.

The first editor of the *Columbian* was probably Mathew Carey. Lyon Richardson maintains that the phrase "these independent and highly favored republics" which appeared in the early advertisements of the magazine, was "characteristic of Carey's early antifederal conception of the Union. . . ." [30] Richardson's opinion is supported by an advertisement in the *Pennsylvania Packet* in September 1786 which stated that "THE EDITOR of the *Columbian Magazine* shall esteem it a very particular Favour, if any Gentleman will furnish him with Anecdotes, or Documents, for writing the Life of that much regretted HERO, GENERAL GREENE". Carey's authorship of the life of Greene, which appeared in the September and the October 1786 *Columbian*, is attested by his including it in his *Miscellaneous Trifles* in 1796.

[30] *Early American Magazines,* 278.

In addition, two other pieces of Carey's appeared in the September issue: "The Shipwreck" and "Hard Times". So it seems probable that he did edit the magazine, at least for the first issue or two, although it is also possible, as Mott suggests, that the other partners had a hand in the editorial work.[31]

Carey's tenure as editor naturally terminated when he withdrew to found the *American Museum*. Apparently, before resigning, Carey attempted to find a replacement for himself. In January 1787, a Mr. M. Clarkson of Philadelphia suggested to Carey that Jeremy Belknap would be the proper man for the job, and Carey discussed the possibility with Belknap's friend Ebenezer Hazard. After some indecision over salary and responsibilities and some discussion in which Trenchard apparently opposed the move, the proprietors offered Belknap the job at 100 pounds a year including whatever writing he might do for the magazine. Belknap refused because of the insufficiency of the salary, although Spotswood had offered him an additional 50 pounds to edit the *Evening Herald*, Hazard had assured him 60 pounds a year as librarian at Carpenter's Hall, and Carey had guaranteed additional money for contributions to the *Museum*. Hazard had earlier told Belknap that "a plain but decent" style of living in Philadelphia would cost 400 pounds a year; and Belknap decided that his salary as pastor of the Federal Street Church in Boston and the money promised him as subscription agent and contributor to both the *Columbian* and the *Museum* made remaining in Boston to his advantage.[32]

After Carey failed to obtain Belknap's services and withdrew from the magazine, Spotswood turned to Francis Hopkinson. Hopkinson, on April 14, 1787, wrote to his friend Thomas Jefferson that he had taken the *Columbian* editorship beginning with the March issue. Described by V. L. Parrington as "a charmingly versatile dilettante", Hopkinson seemed possessed of a breadth of interest and knowledge that would qualify him ideal-

---

[31] *A History of American Magazines*, I, 94.

[32] For the exchange of letters in which Belknap's prospective editorship of the *Columbian* is discussed, see "Belknap Papers", 5th Ser., II, 450-454 and III, 112 and 6th Ser., IV, 329.

ly for the job of magazine editor. A lawyer and jurist by profession, he was also a talented painter, musician, and composer; an amateur scientist who dabbled in astronomy, mathematics, chemistry, physics, and practical invention; a literary man known throughout the colonies for his Revolutionary satires "A Pretty Story" and "The Battle of the Kegs"; and a politician who had signed the Declaration of Independence, been a member of both Continental Congresses, and befriended the founders of the new nation.[33] His literary ability, personal influence, and wide range of knowledge would seem to justify the publishers' hopes that his efforts would immensely improve the magazine.

Unfortunately, Hopkinson's dilettantism impaired his effectiveness as an editor. More interested in politics and society than in procuring fresh literary material for the *Columbian,* he was a great disappointment to Spotswood, who complained in April that all the magazine needed "to give it permanency . . . is a capable editor, who will take its interests warmly in hands, by supplying it with as many original pieces as possible, and when extracts are given, to be from new works, or from old ones that are not generally known".[34] This, Hopkinson failed to do.

How long Hopkinson continued as editor and who succeeded him are disputed questions. Certainly, as Lyon Richardson pointed out, both Frank Luther Mott and George E. Hastings are incorrect in stating that Hopkinson was still editor in 1788, for Alexander James Dallas was definitely editor in September, 1787; but Richardson offers no suggestions as to Hopkinson's successor.[35]

An exchange of correspondence among Spotswood, Jeremy Belknap, and Ebenezer Hazard identifies the new editor. On April 16, 1787, Spotswood informed Belknap that "a Gentleman in this city" had been named editor of the *Columbian* at 150 pounds a year. Belknap, apparently annoyed that the new man

---

[33] The standard biography of Hopkinson is George Everett Hastings, *Life and Writings of Francis Hopkinson* (Chicago, 1926).

[34] "Belknap Papers", 6th Ser., IV, 331.

[35] See Richardson, *Early American Magazines,* 280-281; Mott, *History of American Magazines,* I, 94 and Hastings, *Life of Hopkinson,* 433-434.

(Hopkinson) was getting more money than he had been offered, wrote to Hazard on May 4 asking the identity of the new editor. In a letter dated May 12, Hazard replied: "*I am told* their editor is a John O'Connor, Esq., an Irish counsellor at law. If he is, I do not wonder that 'a *capable* editor is *now* wanted'; for I have no great opinion of *his* abilities." [36] This correspondence seems to suggest that O'Connor was the editor of whom Spotswood wrote Belknap in April; but we know from Hopkinson's April 14 letter to Jefferson that he was in fact editor two days before Spotswood's letter to Belknap. This might lead to the conclusion advanced by Richardson that Hazard was mistaken and O'Connor never edited the magazine.[37] But the most probable solution is that during the three weeks that passed between Spotswood's letter of April 16 and Hazard's of May 4, O'Connor had replaced Hopkinson as editor.

Several pieces of internal and external evidence suggest the probability of this conjecture. A large number of Hopkinson's pieces appeared in the *Columbian* during March, April, and May 1787; but their appearance stopped abruptly after the May issue. On May 12, the Federal Constitutional Convention, to which Hopkinson was a delegate, began meeting in Philadelphia, and Hopkinson immediately entered a violent pamphlet war with the antifederalist faction.[38] It seems likely that Hopkinson, in antici-pation of the convention battle, would have resigned from the *Columbian* early in May and that O'Connor would have been named editor before Hazard's letter to Belknap on May 4. A letter from Francis Childs to Benjamin Franklin tells us that O'Connor was in Philadelphia seeking literary employment in late December 1786 and that Franklin distrusted him.[39] Further-more, the June 1787 issue of the *Columbian* contains the only two pieces related to Ireland and the Irish in the more than six-year history of the magazine. One is a "genuine letter from a

[36]   "Belknap Papers", 5th Ser., II, 474 and 477.
[37]   *Early American Magazines*, 281.
[38]   Charles R. Hildeburn, "Francis Hopkinson", *Pennsylvania Magazine of History and Biography*, II (1878), 324.
[39]   Luther S. Livingston, *Franklin and his Press at Passy* (New York, 1914), 160-162.

native of Ireland" written in Latin during the Revolution to relatives back home. The other is "An Interesting Law Case" dealing with a court decision during the time of William Penn and introduced by an anonymous author who characterizes himself as an itinerant Irish lawyer whose hobby is collecting odd law cases. The description fits O'Connor. In a four-page "Proposal for Printing by Subscription a Geographical and Topographical History of America" written in the fall of 1787, he characterized himself as "a Barrister at Law in the Kingdom of Ireland, and now a Traveller in America". Moreover, in the proposal O'Connor described himself as now "Totally detached from every Occupation. . . ." On the basis of this evidence and of Hazard's letter it seems safe to conclude that O'Connor became editor sometime in May and edited at least the June issue.

O'Connor edited the *Columbian* for no more than one or two issues before he was replaced, probably for incompetence. Alexander James Dallas took up the job, perhaps as early as July 1787. Sometime during that month Belknap had asked Hazard for information concerning Dallas: apparently he had heard either that Dallas was editor or was being considered for the job. In September Belknap referred to "the editor Dallas" with whom he was corresponding about contributions to the magazine.[40] The probability that Dallas became editor in July is supported by the appearance in the July *Columbian* of his "Address Delivered by Mr. Hallam, at the Theatre in Philadelphia, previous to an Entertainment presented on the 25th day of June, 1787, for the benefit of the American Captives of Algiers", one of several prologues Dallas wrote for his friend actor Lewis Hallam, Jr.,[41] and the first of several of his poems to appear in the magazine during his tenure as editor.

Dallas's knowledge of literature and his editorial experience made him one of the best qualified editors of the *Columbian*. He had studied literature and law at Edinburgh University, where he

---

[40] "Belknap Papers", 5th Ser., II, 483 and 489.
[41] The standard life of Dallas is George Mifflin Dallas, *The Life and Writings of A. J. Dallas* (Philadelphia, 1871). For Dallas's friendship with Hallam see p. 15.

attracted the attention of Benjamin Franklin. In 1783 he moved from his native Jamacia to Philadelphia, seeking a climate more favorable to his wife's ill health. In Philadelphia, he took up the study of American law and in 1785 was admitted to the bar before the Supreme Court of Pennsylvania. As he continued to study law, he supported his family by editing the *Columbian* and the *Pennsylvania Evening Herald* for Spotswood.

Dallas edited the magazine for the next year and a half, giving it its second longest period of editorial stability. He made only minor changes in the format. In July 1787 he divided the "Intelligence" section into "Foreign" and "Domestic" (the latter became "American" in April 1788). In the September, November, and December 1788 issues he added a "Law Budget", a summary of the decisions of the Pennsylvania courts, combining his study of law and his editorial duties. The most significant of Dallas's additions was Jeremy Belknap's "American Plutarch" series during 1788. Belknap's biographies of famous Americans appeared as the lead articles in all but one issue during that year and greatly increased the *Columbian's* reputation as a magazine printing original American material.

When Spotswood sold the magazine to Trenchard in December 1788, Dallas resigned as editor. In late November either Spotswood or Trenchard had again offered the editorship to Jeremy Belknap, but he had again refused and recommended Spotswood for the position. Spotswood thanked Belknap for his suggestion, but argued that his talents were insufficient to the task. Trenchard finally hired a new editor in early 1789. On March 7, Hazard wrote to Belknap: "The man you tell me is now editor is a man of genius, a violent Anti-fed., poor as Job, proud as Lucifer, and of a quick and most outrageous temper." [42] Since Belknap's original letter naming the man has disappeared and no other evidence exists as to his identity, Trenchard's editor has remained anonymous. At any rate, he edited no more than four issues, for in June the magazine informed the public that "The

[42] "Belknap Papers", 5th Ser., III, 108. The correspondence in which Belknap is offered the editorship is found in *Ibid.*, 5th Ser., II, 77-78 and 6th Ser., IV, 429.

gentleman who has, for some time past, acted as editor of this magazine, having declined, such communications as were in his hands, are delivered to his successor". The successor was probably Trenchard himself. From June through the end of the year Belknap mentioned only Trenchard in connection with forwarding material to the magazine, and in October Hazard indicated that Trenchard alone was carrying the editorial load.[43]

In an attempt to improve the magazine, Trenchard and his anonymous editor made several changes in the format. In January 1789, they announced that:

the plan is now extended, without any additional expense to the subscribers. Instead of 54 pages of letterpress, originally given, each number shall, in future contain 60 at least; and be embellished with not less than two copper-plates, occasionally coloured for the better illustration of particular objects. The work will be printed on fine paper, with an handsome type, cast on purpose in Philadelphia; and it is determined to publish it punctually on the first day of each succeeding month.

This plan was generally followed. Since he made the engravings himself, saving the cost of having them done, Trenchard did supply three in the January and November issues and four in February, but none was colored. Each issue under his editorship had more pages and fewer articles. This change improved the quality of the publication, for each article was longer and more complete than had been the case in the past. Another important change was the beginning of a serialized history of the Revolution in March 1789, which continued throughout the life of the magazine. This feature was calculated to buttress the *Columbian's* image as a national periodical, and it proved to be a popular addition.

William Spotswood apparently edited the three issues which he published from December 1789 through February 1790. If so, his work bears out his earlier statement to Belknap that he did not possess the talent to edit a magazine. Rather than the longer,

---

[43] *Ibid.*, 5th Ser., III, 201. Benjamin Lewis, *A Register of the editors, printers, and publishers of American Magazines 1741-1810*, 33 concludes that Trenchard edited the magazine during this time.

more complete articles of Trenchard's editorship, Spotswood printed short, chopped-up excerpts clipped from other journals. The "Columbian Parnassiad" shrunk to one or two pages of short, dull verse. The only item of interest during these months was the continuation of the history of the Revolution which Trenchard began. Many months of Spotswood's editorship would have doomed the magazine.

The *Columbian* needed fresh editorial ideas and got them when William Young took over the newly named *Universal Asylum and Columbian Magazine* in March 1790. In Young's hands the publication underwent several significant changes in format. The monthly issues were expanded to 64 pages, including one copperplate by the new engravers James Thackara and John Vallance and one piece of music. The new editor stipulated, however, that "should either the engraving or musick be omitted, 8 additional pages shall be given in lieu thereof; and should both be left out, at any time, the *Asylum*, for that month, shall contain 80 pages" (March 1790, p. 131).

A second change resulted from a compromise of the proprietors' commitment to the old policy of printing foreign and domestic news and the *Philadelphia Magazine's* promise to print an account of the proceedings of the Congress. In July 1790 the editors began to cut the amount of foreign news appearing in the "Chronicle" (formerly the "Intelligence") and to replace it with the full text of governmental documents such as the addresses of the President to Congress and detailed reports by various cabinet members on such national problems as the banks, foreign trade, domestic manufactures, the Indian wars, and trouble with the Algerine pirates. This policy gave the magazine a more narrowly nationalistic look and concentrated the readers' attention on the central issues facing the nation. In June 1791 foreign news resumed, making the "Chronicle" disproportionately long. But in August a new section, the "Political Register", was created to contain the governmental documents, making the *Columbian* the first American magazine to devote a separate section to the printing of governmental papers. This format continued until May 1792, when Young placed at the end of each issue a separately numbered twenty-four page "Appendix of the Acts of the First Session of the Second Congress of the United States". In June, the "Political Register", which had been superseded by the "Appendix", was dropped, only to appear again in September, this time containing documents concerning the French Revolution. This interest in the revolution in France is another indication of the growing nationalistic emphasis which Young gave the magazine, for he directly related the principles guiding European revolutions to the republican principles and national destiny of the United States. By making the magazine a repository of the living history of the new nation, Young greatly increased its prestige and incremented its announced role as the periodical of American nationalism.

A third change, also aimed at strengthening the magazine's American emphasis, was the beginning in June 1790 of the first successful monthly book review column to appear in an American magazine. Although Franklin had attempted a review column in his *General Magazine*, his efforts, and those of his successors, failed after one or two issues. The *Columbian's* "Impartial Review of Late American Publications", which ran from June 1790 till the magazine's death, survived longer than any monthly review column until Charles Brockden Brown's *Monthly Magazine and American Review* in 1799.[44] In announcing the beginning of the "Impartial Review", Young stated that it was considered "an important part of the work" and promised that it would "be continued with strict impartiality, and agreeably to the best judgment of the editors . . . and as the proprietors intend to make it *a permanent basis* on which *a more extensive Review* may be established, at some future period, the utmost pains shall be taken to render it as interesting, complete, and satisfactory as possible" (July 1790, pp. i-ii). Although the review column was never enlarged, it did lay the groundwork for public acceptance of later American review periodicals such as Brown's *Monthly Review* and Joseph Dennie's *Port Folio*; and, since it was the first regularly conducted review column to examine American books ex-

---

[44]   See Mott, *A History of American Magazines*, I, 219.

clusively, it gave the pursuit of letters in the United States a prestige which it had not attained before.

Young's additions to the format of the magazine gave it a new look of stability and a new national spirit which made it, as Frank Luther Mott has stated, "distinctly more solid and serious" in appearance. The continuation of the history of the Revolution, the inclusion of lengthy biographies of American public figures such as Benjamin Franklin, and the publication of governmental papers made it "a precursor of the special historical magazine".[45] The infusion of fresh ideas through the "Society of Gentlemen" and William Young's editorship revived the magazine from the doldrums in which it had floundered during Spotswood's last efforts and earned it almost three full years of continued public support.

III

The chief difficulty that the successive editors of the *Columbian* faced was obtaining suitable material for print. Most Americans still regarded authorship, particularly of belles lettres, with Puritan disapproval; moreover, hewing farms from the wilderness, forging a federal government, and establishing the commercial solvency of the United States left little time for literary activities. Howard Mumford Jones has recently argued that many of the nation's cultured elite were Loyalists and withdrew from the country at the end of the Revolution, thus altering the course of later cultural development.[46] In addition, Republican culture could not provide the leisure necessary for pursuing the fine arts, and a class of professional authors was a luxury the nation could not afford.[47] Carey's *Museum* avoided the problem by establishing itself frankly as a reprint journal. Most of the other magazines of the period stole with less candor from one another and from English periodicals. But the *Columbian* attempted to realize its

45   *Ibid.*, 98-99.
46   *O Strange New World*, 316.
47   *History of American Magazines*, I, 14.

promise to print the best original American pieces available, struggled to find suitable material where it could, and took from other printed sources like the rest when originality was not offered.

In general the magazine used three methods of getting material: by employing paid contributors, by soliciting contributions from the reading public, and by clipping excerpts from other publications. The paid contributors were men whose livelihood did not depend upon literature, but who were sufficiently dedicated to their art to contract with the publishers to produce quality material for pay. The contributors who answered the magazine's public solicitation were of three types: literary amateurs to whom writing was one of the social graces; aspiring young professionals like Charles Brockden Brown, for whose early writings the *Columbian* provided an outlet; and educated gentry whose specialized interest in such varied fields as agriculture, medicine, and science led them to present the fruits of their research in the form of essays. The excerpts came from whatever sources the editors could pillage.

The *Columbian* was the first American magazine regularly to pay for contributions to its pages and was, in a sense, the first professional outlet for periodical literature in the United States. In previous magazines, the only paid contributor was the editor, who supplied material in addition to his editorial services for his salary. Two men, Jeremy Belknap and Benjamin Rush, can be definitely identified as paid contributors to the *Columbian*. A third, Henry Stuber probably was paid for his work, and several others may have received pay.

Jeremy Belknap's contributions to the *Columbian* were so important that Ebenezer Hazard, with justice, believed that "If it lives, I think it will owe its life to you".[48] In each of the nineteen issues between June 1787 and December 1788, Belknap's work appeared as the lead or the second article, and on five occasions each of the first two pieces was his. Ten of the twelve issues in 1789 contained articles by him. These contributions

---

[48]   "Belknap Papers", 5th Ser., III, 59.

were the most extensive body of original American material written by a contributor other than the editor for any eighteenth-century American magazine. The serialization of his novel "The Foresters" over a six-month period in 1787 and 1788 was the first such publication of fiction in the history of American magazines and set the precedent for subsequent serial publication by Charles Brockden Brown, Herman Melville, W. D. Howells, Henry James, and many others. Belknap also contributed biographies of John Winthrop, Sir Fernando Gorges, Captain John Smith, and William Penn; [49] topographical descriptions; excerpts from seventeenth-century American publications generally unavailable at the time and chronicling such diverse subjects as the founding of Harvard College, the original system of laws in the Massachusetts Bay Colony, and a defense of bundling which patriotically stated that less hanky-panky occurred in a New England bed than on a French divan. These works, his accounts of current events in Boston, and his excerpts from New England periodicals constituted a considerable percentage of the quality material printed in the *Columbian* from 1787 through 1789.[50]

Belknap became a paid contributor to the *Columbian* after rejecting the editorship in February 1787. He received a guinea for every three printed pages: thus his contributions appeared in multiples of three pages to simplify bookkeeping. Belknap deducted his pay from the funds he collected as subscription agent

[49] Belknap drew his material from seventeenth-and-early-eighteenth-century histories such as Daniel Neal's *History of the Puritans*, Cotton Mather's *Magnalia Christi Americana*, the anonymous pamphlet *New England's Fruits*, Capt. John Smith's *General History*, and the various historical papers of the colonies of Massachusetts and Pennsylvania which he and Ebenezer Hazard were collecting and publishing.

[50] At the same time Belknap was a paid contributor to the *American Museum*, the *Massachusetts Magazine*, and the *American Magazine*. He may accurately be called America's first free-lance magazine writer. In January 1789 he proposed a merger of the *Columbian, Massachusetts*, and *American* magazines. He felt that uniting the three best American magazines would create a single periodical with originality and quality worthy of the nation. His proposal was rejected, apparently because neither the Boston nor the Philadelphia proprietors felt that subscribers in those cities would read a work printed in the other. See "Belknap Papers", 5th Ser., III, 88-89.

for the magazine. In March 1790, tempting offers from Isaiah Thomas and Noah Webster and the fact that he was apparently unacquainted with the new proprietors of the *Columbian* drew him away from the magazine, and thereafter he contributed no more material.

Belknap should probably share the distinction of being the man who kept the *Columbian* alive with Dr. Benjamin Rush. No less than twenty-five pieces in the magazine can positively be identified as Rush's; and, if he was a member of the "Society of Gentlemen" who published the magazine during its last years, perhaps even more of his writing appeared anonymously. We know from Hazard that Rush was being paid as a contributor in 1789, but he may have worked in that capacity before, perhaps even from the time of the magazine's inception. Rush's first piece appeared in the *Columbian* in November 1786, the third issue of the magazine, and his work continued to appear in profusion through the spring of 1791, at which time he was immobilized by a lung disease from which he did not recover until the summer of 1792.[51] Although some of Rush's pieces, such as "On Female Education" and his commencement address to the Philadelphia medical college, could have been clipped from other publications, the majority seem to have been written originally for the magazine and appeared there for the first time.

When the *Columbian* began publication, Rush was one of the most important literary figures in Philadelphia. His publications on behalf of the Revolution, improved medical care, and various other social causes were known throughout the nation. He was a close friend of Thomas Paine and suggested the title "Common Sense" to Paine. Because he was so closely identified with the founders of the nation, Rush's name signed to contributions gave the *Columbian* an air of dignity and respectability which it needed in its beginning years to appeal to potential contributors and subscribers.

[51] Nathan G. Goodman, *Benjamin Rush, Physician and Citizen* (Philadelphia, 1934), 165-166. Rush's contributions covered a wide field of interest: medicine, education, politics, social studies, satires, eulogies, topographical description, polemics on practical philosophy, and arguments for the abolition of slavery.

Another Philadelphian who may have been a paid contributor was Dr. Henry Stuber. We know little about Stuber beyond the fact that he was born of German parents in Philadelphia in 1770 and received from the University of Pennsylvania the Bachelor of Laws degree in 1784, the Master of Arts in 1787, and the Bachelor of Medicine in 1788. At the university he was a favorite pupil of Dr. Kunze, the noted master of languages. Kunze's influence caused Stuber to forgo the practice of medicine and law and to devote himself to periodical publication while supporting himself with a minor governmental clerkship. Stuber is best known as the author of the first full-length biography of Benjamin Franklin, written after Franklin's death, which was serialized in the *Columbian* from May 1790 to June 1791. None of the other pieces in the magazine can be identified positively as Stuber's, but Benjamin Rush's eulogy on Stuber in the May 1792 *Columbian* suggests that he had contributed extensively to the magazine.[52]

Although the *Columbian* may have paid other contributors, the most common means of getting material was soliciting it from the public. In each annual address to their readers, the publishers renewed their appeal for contributions. Typical is their statement in the *Columbian* for February 1787:

the proprietors are very sensible, that their exertions, alone, must be extremely inadequate to the end proposed: and, as they conceive that the utility of a periodical repository, of this kind, if judiciously managed, is sufficiently obvious to men of understanding, they intreat a continuance of the favors of those gentlemen of genius and science, to whom they are already so much indebted on this score. – They flatter themselves, also, that men of abilities and public spirit, in several states, from whom communications have not yet been received, will be pleased to furnish the Editor, from time to time, with such literary productions of a leisure hour, as may serve to render their magazine more extensively useful. (p. ii)

[52]   For biographical information on Stuber, see Rush's "Account of Henry Stuber", *Columbian* (May 1792), 291-293; Evert A. and George L. Duyckinck, *Cyclopaedia of American Literature* (New York, 1856), I, 107; Gen. Joshua L. Chamberlain, *The University of Pennsylvania* (Boston, 1902), II, 13-14; and Jared Sparks, ed., *The Works of Benjamin Franklin* (Boston, 1847), X, 403-404.

The editors also made specific requests. In April 1787 they asked for articles concerning natural history in the United States. Jeremy Belknap on several occasions resorted to public requests for information relevant to his American Plutarch biographies. During the serialization of the history of the Revolution the editors requested "such gentlemen as are possessed of authentic documents, calculated to throw light upon any part of the subject, and which have not yet been made public, to communicate them". The same request specifically asked for documents which would illuminate the "circumstances which preceeded the *declaration of independence*, and prepared the minds of the people for that memorable event" (November 1790, p. 354). In answer, the editors received a number of the unpublished letters of John Adams, which they printed in March and April 1792. But such solicitation often proved dangerous. When Stuber's life of Franklin was appearing, the editors were forced to comment that the "*Anecdotes of Dr. Franklin*, communicated by Y. Z. seem, like many others which have been attributed to that great man, to be spurious. Some of them certainly do not bear the least resemblance of his manner" (November 1790, p. 282). But such unreliability did not deter the editors from continuing the solicitation.

Solicitation, even when successful, was not foolproof. Pieces were sometimes lost in the mail or arrived too late for insertion in the scheduled issue. Such delays were particularly embarrassing when the work was being serialized. The editor in May 1789 apologized that the "Life of William Penn" was not included and hoped that "Our readers will have the goodness to impute the latter disappointment to the distant residence of the correspondent". During the change of editorship in 1789 many pieces were lost, and apologies appeared for several months thereafter. In October 1788, the editor announced that "A correspondent authorizes us to promise the publication of *An Analytical Chart* of the *New Federal Government* . . .", but the promise was never fulfilled. Another piece was postponed because of "the inattention of the person intrusted with the delivery". (August 1789, p. 448). Even when the material did reach the editor, there were possible snags. In October 1788 they informed the public that "We intended to have published the *Willow of Litchfield* in the present Magazine, but its ingenious author has written in such illegible characters, that the printers could not decypher the manuscript" (p. 548). Another contributor's work was rejected because of "the want of proper types ..." (January 1789, p. 2). But the most irksome habit of contributors was trying to pass off as original, pieces copied from other sources. In November 1790 the editor angrily informed the readers: "The *elegy* signed Z. is not *original*. Did this pretended author suppose we had never read *Shenstone*. – It is a pity that any person would be so extremely weak and vain, as to exult like a *jackadaw*, in stolen plumage" (p. 282). But such invectives had little effect. Less than a year later the editors were begging "Our correspondents, who transmit *selected* articles ... not to give them the *appearance* of *originality*" (April 1791, p. 210).

The *Columbian* offered the authors who answered its solicitations a forum for their amateur productions and gave anonymity to those who wished to escape the stigma of publicly acknowledged authorship. Most wrote under pseudonyms, although some were widely known to the readers. They included most of the men and women who made up the literary culture of Philadelphia during the early national period.

Elizabeth Graeme Fergusson contributed faithfully. She may have been paid, but the lavish acknowledgments of thanks to her in the "Notes to Contributors" suggest that she was not. From September 1787 to September 1792 she sent the editors more than a dozen of her poems, several pieces of prose, the previously unpublished poems of her niece Ann Young Smith, and a letter "On Novel Reading" written by her cousin Deborah Senrich. One of the most cultured women in Pennsylvania, Mrs. Fergusson had long been recognized as Philadelphia's leading poetess. She began her poetic career at the age of seventeen when she translated Fenelon's *Télémaque* into blank verse to relieve the anguish of her broken engagement to William Franklin. After a visit to England, where she was introduced to King George III and became a friend of Laurence Sterne and the celebrated Dr. Fothergill, she began a poetic correspondence with young Philadelphia poet Nathaniel Evans under the pseudonym Laura, which she used for all her contributions to the *Columbian*. After his premature death in 1767, the publication of their poems in the *American Magazine* and in a volume edited by Provost William Smith established her reputation. Her home Graeme Park became the center of Philadelphia culture, and her Saturday salon attracted such men as Benjamin Franklin, Benjamin Rush, Francis Hopkinson, Provost William Smith, and many other literary figures who were her lifelong friends.[53] During the Revolution her husband deserted her to join the Royal Army, she became innocently involved in a Tory plot to end the war, and her estate was confiscated. Only the pleas of her friends Hopkinson and George Meade restored her to official favor. During the time she published in the *Columbian* she was living frugally at Graeme Park, writing, translating the Psalms, and studying theology.

In addition to her own poems, Mrs. Fergusson sent the editors eight poems signed "Sylvia", the work of her niece Ann Young Smith. Just prior to the Revolution Ann Young had married Dr. William Smith of Philadelphia, a physician and 1771 graduate of the medical college. During her husband's service for the colonial cause, Mrs. Smith wrote a number of patriotic poems, a few of which were probably published in Philadelphia newspapers and one of which, "Elegy to the Memory of the American Volunteers", appeared in Tom Paine's *Pennsylvania Magazine*

[53] Benjamin Rush later described the pleasures of such occasions as follows: "she instructed by the stores of knowledge contained in the historians, philosophers, and poets of ancient and modern nations, which she called forth at her pleasure; and again she charmed by a profusion of original ideas, collected by her vivid and widely expanded imagination, and combined with exquisite taste and judgment . . .". "Elizabeth Graeme Fergusson", *Port Folio*, I (June 1809), 523. Many of Mrs. Fergusson's papers are in the collection of the Historical Society of Pennsylvania. Biographical information can be found in Rush; Simon Gratz, "Some Materials for a Biography of Mrs. Elizabeth Fergusson, *nee* Graeme", *Pennsylvania Magazine of History and Biography*, XXXIX (1915), 257-321 and 385-433; Duyckinck, *Cyclopaedia*, I, 232; Ellis Paxson Oberholtzer, *Literary History of Philadelphia* (Philadelphia, 1906), 78; and Moses Coit Tyler, *Literary History of the American Revolution 1763-1783* (New York, 1957), I, 160-162.

in February 1776. After her premature death in 1780, her papers came into the possession of her long-time guardian Elizabeth Graeme Fergusson who sent the eight poems to the *Columbian*.

A number of Philadelphia gentlemen-poets contributed a large body of occasional verse heavy in local allusion. The most energetic of these was John Swanwick, a public figure who was a representative from Pennsylvania in the United States Congress and who would literally address a poem to a young lady at the drop of a handkerchief. The titles of his poems reveal their nature: "To Mrs. Howard, on her Marriage", "Verses Addressed to Miss Anna P - - - ", "To Miss Peggy C - - w, with a bow of ribbons found after a dance, and supposed to belong to that young lady", "On a Walk in Statehouse Yard", and "Lines Written in Bethlehem". His *vers de société* has little literary merit, but was apparently popular gossip for Philadelphia readers.

Peter Markoe, called "the City Poet", contributed three identified poems and probably many other pieces of anonymous verse. The son of a West Indies sugar planter who owned considerable real estate in Philadelphia, Markoe was educated at the University of Dublin, was a lawyer by profession and a writer of occasional verse by habit. His long poem "The Times" was widely reprinted at the end of the century and his tragedy "The Patriot Chief" was popular on the Philadelphia stage. The now-unknown Markoe was so respected in his own time that Noah Webster once called him "one of the first poetical geniuses in America", which is not a unique instance of Webster's talent for aesthetic misjudgment.[54]

Another Philadelphian who contributed both verse and prose to the *Columbian* was Charles Crawford. The heir to a large family fortune from a West Indian plantation, Crawford had achieved a poetical reputation while at Queen's College, Cambridge, with a series of hot-tempered attacks on ancient and

---

[54] *American Magazine* (September 1788), 729. For biographical information on Markoe, see Oberholtzer, 153; and Sister Mary Crysostom Diebels, S. S.N. D., *Peter Markoe (1752?-1792). A Philadelphia Writer* (Catholic University, 1944).

modern philosophers and with his *Sophropia and Hilario: An Ode*, which he published in 1774. Between that time and 1792 he published more than a dozen volumes. His light verse and his essays opposing slavery made him a popular literary figure in Philadelphia. He, like Markoe and Mrs. Fergusson, was recognized as a leader of the Philadelphia literati, and the presence of his poems distinguished the pages of the magazine in the eyes of its readers.[55]

The magazine's best known contributor of prose was Charles Brockden Brown. The *Columbian* gave Brown his first experience with magazine publication and pointed the direction of his later literary career. His four-part periodical essay "The Rhapsodist", which appeared in the magazine in August through November 1789, has been called, mistakenly, his first published work. Brown, a young man of 17, finished Robert Proud's Latin School and entered the law office of *Columbian* contributor Alexander Wilcox in the fall of 1786, when the magazine first began publication. At the same time he began participating in literary activities through the Belles Lettres Club. His first publications appeared in 1789: a poem in the *State Gazette of North Carolina* and "The Rhapsodist" in the *Columbian*.[56] Carl Van Doren speculates that Brown may have published short stories anonymously for several years before he established his *Weekly Magazine* in 1794.[57] If so, he possibly published stories in the *Columbian* in the wake of the favorable editorial reaction to his essays; but none of the many pieces of short fiction in the magazine can be positively identified as his.

Another prominent, if reluctant, contributor to the *Columbian* was John Quincy Adams. Adams's 1787 Harvard Commencement oration so impressed Jeremy Belknap that he wrote Adams

[55] For a detailed treatment of Crawford's career see Lewis Leary, "Charles Crawford, a Forgotten Poet", *Pennsylvania Magazine of History and Biography*, LXXXIII (1959), 293-306.
[56] See Harry R. Warfel, *Charles Brockden Brown* (Gainesville, Fla., 1949), 24-35; and David Lee Clark, *Charles Brockden Brown*, 42-47 for accounts of this period of Brown's career.
[57] "Minor Tales of Charles Brockden Brown", *The Nation*, C (January 14, 1915), 46-47.

requesting a copy to be printed in the *Columbian*. Adams modestly replied that he would consent provided the commencement poem of his classmate Thaddeus Mason Harris also be printed; otherwise, he would refuse, "as it might perhaps be considered as a mark of presumption in me to assume a distinction, which others, much more meritorious, had declined through modesty". Belknap, who had already forwarded Adams's piece to William Spotswood, was embarrassed to find that Harris refused. He then wrote Adams a flattering letter praising the Adams family and suggesting that it is the wisdom of the great to avoid false modesty; Adams replied, leaving publication at Belknap's discretion, asking only that his name be withheld. The oration appeared in September 1787 with Adams's name attached.[58]

Noah Webster twice found occasion to defend himself in the *Columbian*. Not particularly popular anywhere, Webster was anathematized in Philadelphia because of a series of bitter experiences in the city in 1787.[59] The *Columbian* first angered him in September 1788 when it printed Belknap's article correcting Webster's speculation on the origin of Indian fortifications on the bank of the Ohio. Webster protested with a long letter to the

[58]   Mr. Mayo, "Belknap and John Quincy Adams, 1787", *Proceedings of the Massachusetts Historical Society*, LIX (1926), 203-210, contains on account of the episode and reprints the exchange of letters between Belknap and Adams.

[59]   Webster's trouble in Philadelphia began when Franklin asked him to lecture at the University in January 1787. After two weeks public indifference and Pennsylvania snow canceled him. Bitter over his failure, he then made the mistake of engaging popular University President John Ewing in public debate over the government's policy on paper money and was viciously denounced by the press. When he became master of English at the Protestant Episcopal Academy in April, his grammatical experiments brought more vitriolic attacks, including an open letter by James Kidd to the Constitutional Convention demanding that something be done about "the destructive, heretical grammar" spreading "disorder, confusion, and error among the rising generation". The Philadelphia opinion of Webster is aptly expressed by Ebenezer Hazard: "*I* think the *Monarch* is a literary puppy, from what little I have seen of him. He certainly does not want understanding, and yet there is a mixture of self-sufficiency, all-sufficiency, and at the same time a degree of insufficiency about him, which is (to me) intolerable." "Belknap Papers", 5th Ser., III, 23. Also see, Harry Warfel, *Noah Webster: Schoolmaster to America* (New York, 1936), 159-163.

editors, who printed his letter and cynically dismissed it. Then in November 1790 the "Impartial Review" published a vicious attack on Webster's *Fugitiv Essays*. Webster defended his character and his grammatical methods in a long letter printed in the September and October 1791 issues, but his objections were again derided by the editors and he made no further contributions to the magazine.

Although men like Brown, Adams, and Webster were seriously attempting literary careers, the majority of the contributors to the *Columbian* were lawyers, physicians, and politicians, not writers. Most were men of middle age, independent means, and catholic interests. Many had been officers during the Revolution or members of the Continental Congress. They belonged to organizations seriously attempting to further the destiny of the new nation – the American Philosophical Society, the Philadelphia Society for the Promotion of Agriculture, the Society for the Advancement of Manufactures and Commerce, and similar groups. As the ruling gentry of the Middle Atlantic states they were active in support of the most advanced social, political, and scientific causes of their time. They formed the intellectual elite of the nation, the audience to whom the *Columbian* was addressed and from whom it drew most of its material.

Typical of these men was Charles Thompson, whose "Investigations of the Justice of Buffon's Opinion of Man in America" in March 1788 was perhaps the most thoughtful defense of American culture to appear in the *Columbian*. Thompson, who began life as a penniless immigrant, became one of America's first competent Greek scholars (he translated the *Septuagint* and other Greek works) and the owner of a profitable mercantile business. He was elected secretary of the First Continental Congress and during the Revolution was personally in charge of all the correspondence of the Congress.[60]

The experience of the other *Columbian* authors ranged from that of federal geographer Thomas Hutchins, who had early won fame as the planner of Fort Pitt, to Alexander McGillivray, chief

[60] John F. Watson, *Annals of Philadelphia and Pennsylvania in the Olden Times* (Philadelphia, 1855), I, 274-276.

of the Creek Indians, who contributed a description of the Creek Lands to the *Columbian* in 1790 while he was in Philadelphia signing a peace treaty with the United States. But most contributors, whether ministers like Alexander Macwhorter, politicians like François-Xavier Martin and James M'Henry, or businessmen like Thomas Clifford, shared a common background and a common interest in advancing the cause of letters and science in America. Unfortunately, the literary and cultural activities of these men was a cliquish affair in which the average citizen did not participate as reader or writer. This fact alone explains much of the dificulty early American magazines found in obtaining subscribers and original contributions. Because so few men actually engaged in the production of literature, magazines and newspapers were forced to pass what material was available back and forth among themselves, producing periodicals which gave the appearance of being, in one author's words, "sissors and paste pot jobs".

The tradition of the miscellany magazine was that of a reprint journal. The *Gentleman's Magazine*, which served as the model for the *Columbian*, had been established for the purpose of excerpting the most interesting and enlivening features from the many serials and half-sheets which appeared in London during the latter seventeenth and early eighteenth centuries. Walter Graham has pointed out that neither its editor nor publisher conceived of *Gentleman's* as a medium of original publication.[61] Following its example, American magazines from 1741 through 1794 extracted approximately three-fourths of their material from other publications.[62] The *Columbian*, in seeking original material, opposed a tendency so firmly established that its failure was inevitable. On the average, the *Columbian* managed to find a little more than one-fourth original material for each issue, but it was forced to depend for the remainder on pieces clipped from newspapers, other magazines, and books.

The editors of the *Columbian* found New England magazines a particularly fruitful source of material. The *New Haven Gazette,*

⁶¹ *English Literary Periodicals* (New York, 1930), 150.
⁶² *History of American Magazines*, I, 39.

the *Worcester Magazine,* and the *Boston Magazine* reached few readers in the Philadelphia area, so the *Columbian* could assume that the pieces they printed were not widely known to its readers. The work of the Connecticut Wits appealed particularly to the editors since the Hartford group was producing much of the original poetry of quality being written in America at the time. Three poems by Lemuel Hopkins, "The Apostate Apostle", 'The Cancer Quack", and "The Hypocrite's Hope", which first appeared in the *New Haven Gazette* and the *American Mercury* in 1785 and 1786, were appropriated by the *Columbian* in February, March, and May 1787, respectively. In September 1786 and January 1787, the *Columbian* printed three works by David Humphreys: "Mount Vernon. An Ode inscribed to General Washington", "Elegy on the Burning of Fairfield, Connecticut", and the "Letters relative to the treatment of Captain Asgill". A selection from the fifth number of the *Anarchiad* appeared in the magazine less than a month after its first publication in January 1787. The *Columbian* also excerpted portions of Joel Barlow's *Vision of Columbus* and lifted John Trumbull's parody "The Wedding, an Epithalamium", both probably taken from book publication.

David Humphreys was of particular importance to the *Columbian* because of his close connection with General Washington and the Revolution. On the basis of the popular triumph of Humphreys' patriotic poems, Washington had invited him to spend a time at Mount Vernon studying documents for a projected history of the Revolution. From his residence at Mount Vernon came several poems, the Asgill letters, and the material for his life of General Putnam, portions of which appeared in the *Columbian* in October and November 1788. Although now generally unknown, Humphreys was one of the most acclaimed writers of the new nation; his name was mentioned wherever the poetical genius of America was discussed.[63] Publishing his work

---

[63] See, for example, David Ramsay, *History of the American Revolution* (London, 1793), II, 321-322; Joel Barlow, *The Vision of Columbus* (Hartford, 1787), 212; and Samuel Miller, *A Brief Retrospect of the Eighteenth Century* (New York, 1803), II, 230-231.

was almost mandatory for any magazine with nationalistic pre-
tentions.

Periodicals from other parts of the country also provided copy.
The Charleston, South Carolina, *Columbian Herald* yielded
several Ossianic imitations written by Dr. Joseph Brown Ladd,
a physician and poet whose work Lewis Leary has characterized
as "Imitative, pretentious, sentimental, . . . the popular literary
fare on which our ancestors fattened at the end of the eighteenth
century." [64] Other material was taken from a variety of American
newspapers and from the journals of the American Philosophical
Society and the Massachusetts Agricultural Society.[65]

The absence of a national copyright law made American books
fair game for an enterprising editor. Books reviewed in the
"Impartial Review" proved to be one of the most popular sources
of material for the *Columbian*. Typically, the editors would print
excerpts from a book to be reviewed one or two months before
and after the review appeared, usually without crediting the title
or author. For example, an account of the founding of Dartmouth
College was lifted from Belknap's *History of New Hampshire* in
December 1791 and his description of the battle of Louisburg in
January 1792; the review of his book appeared in February,
followed in November by another extract. Extracts from Bartram's
Travels appeared in January and February 1792, preceding the
review in March and April. A review of the first volume of
Modern Chivalry appeared in February 1792, accompanied by
an extract from the novel entitled "H. H. Brackenridge on Indian
Philosophers". After *Modern Chivalry*, volume two, was reviewed
in August 1792, "A Pathetic Story from Modern Chivalry" appeared in September. Along with a review of Francis Hopkinson's

---

[64] "Forgotten Charleston Poet: Joseph Brown Ladd, 1764-1786", *Americana*, XXXVI (1942), 581. Another sketch of Ladd's life can be found in
The Literary Remains of Joseph Brown Ladd, ed. W. B. Chittenden (New
York, 1832).
[65] There appears to have been a particularly close connection between
the *Columbian* and the American Philosophical Society. Most of the men
who published and edited the magazine were also officers of the Society,
and the *Early Proceedings of the American Philosophical Society* (Philadelphia, 1884) often records that articles which were rejected for publication in the Society's *Transactions* were forwarded to the *Columbian*.

three-volume *Works* in August 1792, the editors printed one of the essays and several of the poems from the book. The practice was applied to almost every book reviewed in the magazine.

The editors were always alert to material of topical interest. In May, June, and July 1792, while they were giving extensive coverage of the French Revolution, they printed long excerpts from Thomas Paine's *Rights of Man* and several letters which Paine had written Benjamin Rush from the Bastille. In November 1792 they printed a long letter by Gilbert Imlay on the soil of Kentucky and navigation of the Mississippi River which they had taken from his book *A Topographical Description of the Western Territory of North America* published in London in 1792. This rare description of the far frontier was a prized bit of Americana which capitalized on the growing national concern for the western lands. In addition, the editors did not recoil from printing manuscripts not intended for publication. When extracts from Jefferson's then unpublished *Notes on Virginia* appeared in the April and May 1787 issues, the author wrote to John Stockdale:

unless you are very sure of your information of the printing of the Notes on Virginia in America, I doubt it. I never sent but six copies to America, and they were in such hands as I am sure would not permit them to be published. ... On the contrary, Mr. Hopkinson, one of those to whom I had given a copy, and who is concerned in compiling the Columbian magazine, tells me he hopes I will not object to his publishing a few extracts from it.[66]

Jefferson apparently did not know that Hopkinson had already printed the extracts and was asking his belated permission.

The *Columbian* printed a number of Benjamin Franklin's letters and other writings. Many of them appeared for the first time in America in the magazine's pages. The first wave of Franklin papers came immediately after the magazine began publication, no doubt because of the friendship of Franklin and *Columbian* editor Mathew Carey. On August 10, 1786, when he was preparing the first issues of the magazine, Carey wrote to

---

[66] *Catalogue of the Library of Thomas Jefferson*, E. Millicent Sowerby, compiler (Washington, D. C., The Library of Congress, 1959), V, 157-159.

Franklin asking permission to print the first part of Franklin's manuscript memoirs. Franklin replied that "The memoirs you mention would be of little or no use to your scheme, as they contain only some notes of my early life and finish in 1730. They were written to my son, and intended only as information to my family." Franklin went on to state that he intended to leave a finished autobiography at his death, and "in the meantime I wish nothing of the kind may be published, and shall be much obliged to the proprietors of the *Columbian Magazine* if they will drop that intention for the present".[67] Although he honored Franklin's wishes and dropped plans to publish the memoirs, Carey did print three of the bagatelles in the early issues of the magazine: "The Deformed and Handsome Leg" and "The Art of Procuring Pleasant Dreams" in October and "The Morals of Chess" in December 1786. These bagatelles appeared anonymously, addressed "To the Editors of the Columbian Magazine", who implied that they were written especially for the magazine and not at an earlier date. Carey's access to the bagatelles can be explained by the fact that he worked as a typesetter for Franklin's press at Passy in 1779, the year Franklin began to compose the bagatelles and to print them on his private press for distribution among his friends. Carey was familiar with all of Franklin's unpublished writings and used that familiarity advantageously in his various periodical ventures.[68]

The *Columbian* printed a second group of Franklin papers beginning in the month of Franklin's death, April 1790 and continuing through November 1790, and a third group in May and August 1792. Most of these pieces had been published previously, and their appearance in the *Columbian* coincided with the publi-

[67] *Complete Works of Benjamin Franklin*, ed. John Bigelow (New York, 1888), IX, 332-333.

[68] Carey later printed three other bagatelles, "A Petition of the Left Hand", "The Whistle", and "The Ephemera" in the *American Museum* in May and October 1790. Paul Leicester Ford, *A Franklin Bibliography* (Brooklyn, N. Y., 1889), 289 identifies the appearance of the three bagatelles in the *Museum*, but does not notice the first three in the *Columbian*. Richard Amacher, *Franklin's Wit and Folly* (New Brunswick, N. J., 1953) comments on the appearance of all six, but does not link the three in the *Columbian* to Carey.

cation of a great mass of Franklin material in American magazines at the time of his death.

Another American manuscript published for the first time in the *Columbian* was William Byrd II's "A Description of the Dismal Swamp, in Virginia; with Proposals for and Observations on the Advantages of draining it", which appeared in April 1789. How the Byrd manuscript reached the *Columbian* editors can only be guessed. When the piece was reprinted in the *Farmer's Register* in 1837, a note said that the editors had received the manuscript in Byrd's own handwriting from George E. Harrison of Brandon, Virginia. When William Byrd III died, he willed the entire Byrd literary property, including his father's manuscripts, to his wife Mary Willing Byrd, originally of a prominent Philadelphia family. Mrs. Byrd arranged to have the Byrd library sold at auction in Philadelphia in 1788 and returned to the Quaker City to visit or to live at that time.[69] She probably brought with her the manuscript of "A Description of the Dismal Swamp", which she later willed, along with the Westover Manuscript of the *Secret History of the Dividing Line*, to her daughter Evelyn Taylor Byrd Harrison, grandmother of George E. Harrison from whom the *Farmer's Register* got the manuscript in 1837. No doubt some friend of Mrs. Byrd's connected with the *Columbian* persuaded her to allow the publication of the "Description" in the magazine. Its appearance in the *Columbian* in April 1789 marks the first publication of any of Byrd's writing about the Dismal Swamp and the Dividing Line episode.

Despite the editors' efforts, the accumulated corpus of American writing proved too small to sustain a monthly publication. The editors' refusal to print any material which would be familiar to their Philadelphia readers forced them to raid foreign publications in order to have enough material for their issues. Fiction from the *Universal Magazine* and articles from *Gentleman's Magazine*, the *London Magazine,* the *Analytical Review*, and *La Gazette* of Paris appeared frequently, along with extracts from the journals

[69]   Edwin Wolf, 2nd, "The Dispersal of the Library of William Byrd of Westover", *Proceedings of the American Antiquarian Society* (April 16, 1957-October 15, 1958), 19-106.

of the London Society for the Encouragement of Art, Manufactures and Commerce, the Irish Academy of Arts and Sciences, the Manheim Meteorological Society, and the Bath Society of Agriculture, Art and Science. Excerpts from the French Encyclopedists and from European travel narratives proved particularly popular. Paradoxically, an intense interest in other nations paralleled the demand for a uniquely American culture. Accounts from such works as Father Falkner's *Account of the Patagonians*, Grellamann's *Dissertation on the Gypsies*, De Lazowski's *Tour in Switzerland*, Bruce's *Travels in Africa*, Philip Carteret's *Voyage Around the World*, Knox's *Tour of the Hebrides*, Vaillant's *Travels in Africa*, Abate Toderini's *History of Turkish Literature*, and Abbe Grosier's *Description of China* appealed to the growing American habit of defining the excellence of its own culture by contrasting it to the degeneracy of others, for most excerpts measured foreign institutions against republican standards and found them wanting. Extracts from Du Pratz's *History of Louisiana*, Beattie's *Journal in America*, and Keysler's *Travels* gave Americans an image of their own land through foreign eyes.[70] These clippings from foreign publications show the same sensitivity to foreign criticism of America that was later manifested in the American reaction to English visitors like Dickens, Arnold, and Mrs. Trollope.

Although many foreign works did appeal to Americans, the majority were used for filler. Most of the pieces clipped from English periodicals were printed anonymously and were not identified as English. Less enterprising editors such as William

---

[70]   This diverse array of foreign books was readily available in Philadelphia. Howard Mumford Jones, "The Importation of French Books in Philadelphia, 1750-1800", *Studies in Philology*, XXVIII (October, 1931), 235-251 points out that the *Memoirs of Baron de Tott* and Vaillant's *Travels in Africa*, to mention only two European books from which the *Columbian* clipped, were advertised by Philadelphia booksellers from 1784 through 1788. Scott H. Goodnight makes an equally good case for the easy availability of German books in Philadelphia in his *German Literature in American Magazines*, University of Wisconsin Bulletin, Philology and Literature Series, Vol. IV, No. 1 (Madison, 1907). Advertisements by the booksellers who were partners in the *Columbian* include many of the books from which the editors took extracts.

Spotswood found it necessary to rely heavily on such material, and, as a result, the magazine declined noticeably in their hands. There were simply not enough Americans writing enough printable material to sustain a group of monthly magazines during this period. Had Jeremy Belknap's proposal of merging the *Columbian, Massachusetts,* and *American* magazines succeeded, perhaps America could have produced a single periodical with sufficient capital, capable editorship, and talented contributors to hasten the beginning of a national literature, but regional jealousies doomed his plan, and money and ability continued to be spread too thin. The amazing thing about the *Columbian* is that it managed to persevere so long and so well against such overwhelming handicaps.

The six-year struggle to keep the *Columbian Magazine* alive is symptomatic of one cause of the failure of American literary nationalism in its first period. The season for the flowering of American culture had not come. The number of citizens possessing education and money enough to support a quality literary magazine was too small to make it a profitable venture. Only the upper class received an education that would likely develop a taste in literature. The vast majority of the middle and lower classes were apprenticed to trades or received no education at all.[71] Of the educated upper class, the number intelligent and talented enough to produce competent literary works was even smaller. The most able were attracted to the practical problems of government. Thomas Jefferson, James Madison, and John Quincy Adams, perhaps the most literate and talented men of their generation, devoted their lives to public service and had little leisure for the cultivation of the arts. The great bulk of literature was produced by the ever-present amateur whose dedication was weak and talent weaker. Moreover, the nation faced a desperate financial crisis as the result of the depreciation of Continental paper money and the presence of a large war debt. Investment in magazines to encourage a national literature was a luxury which the nation could not afford in the 1780's. And, although an

[71] Nye, *The Cultural Life of the New Nation*, 152.

appreciative audience is not prerequisite to the creation of literature, it is an historical fact that no period of literary greatness has flourished without healthy media and interested audiences. Such a condition existed in America after the 1830's, but in the 1780's practical affairs pressed too heavily upon cultured Americans to make possible the realization of a classical greatness in art.

II

AMERICAN IDEALS AND BRITISH CRITICISM

Although the editors of the *Columbian Magazine* announced no official critical policy, we can deduce their literary beliefs from the comments made in the "Notes to Contributors" which prefaced each issue and from the judgments made in the "Impartial Review". One explanation for the poor quality of American writing during the early national period is that writers, editors, and publishers accepted literary theories which stifled imagination and reduced literary creativity to the mechanical application of dogmatic rules.[1] The rules which Boileau, Pope, and the other neoclassical critics observed in the Greek and Roman classics existed to check the excesses of the metaphysical imagination and to provide an artistic form within which nature became meaningful. Pope instructed the writer and critic to "First follow NATURE, and your Judgment frame / By her just Standard . . ." ("Essay on Criticism", 11, 68-69). After nature came the rules which methodized it and subjected it to form. Nature without form was a chaos of meaningless observations, the very antithesis of art; rules without nature produced dull and bloodless scholastic exer-

---

[1] Leon Howard describes the stifling effect of neoclassical literary theory on the post-Revolutionary American imagination as follows: ". . . the products of their enthusiasm, study, and sensitivity are generally imitative in form, neoclassic in style, and deadly in their effect upon sensitive later readers. The contradiction implicit in a literature which was original in intent yet imitative in effect, romantic in substance yet neoclassic in form, is a fourth obstacle to the satisfactory description of this period in the conventional terminology of literary history." "The Late Eighteenth Century", *Transitions in American Literary History*, 53. Professor Howard here states in general terms the contradiction which this study attempts to document in detail from the pages of one magazine.

cises in rhetoric. Both these extremes Pope wished to avoid. Unfortunately, by the end of the eighteenth century, slavish imitation of rules and models of excellence had superseded nature in much of English criticism and literature. The *Columbian Magazine* formed its critical opinions on the corpse of neoclassicism embalmed by Scotch common sense realism.

The most frequently used critical terms in the *Columbian* are morality, universality, decorum, sublimity, and correctness. What these words meant to the magazine can be found in the dogmatic codification which the Scotch realists imposed on neoclassical criticism. During the period in which the *Columbian* was being published, Scotch rhetorician Hugh Blair's *Lectures on Rhetoric and Belles Lettres* was the standard text in American universities, and, along with the more theoretical *Elements of Criticism* by Henry Home, Lord Kames, dominated American critical thought.[2] Although both Blair and Kames were consistent with neoclassical taste and were "an obvious extension of similar ideas in Longinus, Boileau, Pope, and all their descendants",[3] they differed from their predecessors in two respects: first, they categorized the elements of rhetoric according to the preconceived emotional effects they would likely produce and, secondly, they asserted dogmatically that taste is formed by conformity to the universal "common sense" of man as a species.[4] The belief in a single standard of taste in all people denied the individual play of the artist's imagination, and the belief that specific rhetorical figures touched the common taste in consistent ways made literature a mechanical game much like the present creation of poetry by electronic computer. Thus, while the editors of the *Columbian* insisted on the free play of nationalistic imagination, they accepted critical dogmas that restricted the exercise of imagination

---

[2]   William Charvat, *The Origins of American Critical Thought 1810-1835* (New York, 1961), 31 ff. establishes the influence of Blair and Kames and traces the effect of that influence on the later period.

[3]   Samuel H. Monk, *The Sublime: A Study of Critical Theories in XVIII-Century England* (New York, Modern Language Association of America, 1935), 116.

[4]   Most American men of letters at this time would have known the discussion of common sense and taste found in Lord Kames, *Elements of Criticism* (Edinburgh, 1788), Chapter XXV.

to a narrowly defined field. While they demanded uniquely American writing, they approved only "the true Attic Salt", mined according to the rules, as seasoning for the American literary palate.[5]

The first demand that the editors of the *Columbian* made of any piece was that it teach a moral lesson. Professor W. J. Bate believes that "the classical and Renaissance conception of the poet as a teacher of moral excellence" was implicit in all neoclassical literary criticism.[6] Although neither Pope, Addison, nor Johnson advocated complete didacticism, Hugh Blair in 1777 insisted that "the ultimate end of all poetry, indeed, of every composition, should be to make some useful impression on the mind".[7] The traditional Puritan emphasis on morality gave American critics an even stronger didactic bent than their English counterparts. The editors of the *Columbian* stated most explicitly in June 1791 that literature should teach "in a way suited to attract the attention of all classes of readers, the most pure and sublime precepts of morality. Unless thus rendered subservient to the interest of virtue, compositions . . . are unworthy of attention. However distinguished by harmony of language, of richness and variety of imagery, they are but a *splendid nothing*." Blair's influence is obvious.

Both the editors of and the contributors to the *Columbian* accepted didacticism as *a priori* to literary achievement. The demand for morality was so strong that several books reviewed in the magazine were recommended for their moral content despite defective style.[8] But the absence of moral purpose meant certain rejection of any composition. The editors were often caustic: "R. W.'s *History of the Times* affords a lamentable proof

---

[5] The "Notes to Contributors" in January 1791, p. 2 condemned a poem for not being seasoned with "the true Attic salt".

[6] *From Classic to Romantic* (New York, Harper and Brothers, 1961), 4. Professor Bate traces in detail the similarity of the critical theories of Blair and Kames to the earlier neoclassical period, 94-113.

[7] Hugh Blair, *Lectures on Rhetoric and Belles Lettres* (Dublin, 1786), II, 239.

[8] See, for example, the review of "*Notes on the last Illness, and Death of a most beloved Friend*" (October 1790), 264 ff.

of the existence of strong intellectual powers, unconnected with every principle of *morality* . . ." they wrote in January 1791; and in May of the same year, "the humor of 'The Nunnery' is not sufficient to atone for the *poison to morals* with which it is accompanied".

The editors encouraged imitating good writers, but they warned their contributors against unwholesome models. They deplored particularly the influence of Goethe's Werther and of Sheridan's Charles Surface as poisonous to morals. To one imitator of Sheridan the editors remarked: "Whatever may have a tendency to bring into disrepute those habits of industry, honesty, and sobriety, which characterize the members of every well-regulated society; whatever holds out idleness, injustice, and extravagance, as exemplary and praise-worthy, is too dangerous to be promulgated" (June 1791, p. 330). To another they observed that such a hero "might well have a claim upon our *pity*; but, it is not by artful glossing over his offences that he can be entitled to a share of our *esteem*. In order to this [sic], he must appear to be truly virtuous, which he never can, while he endeavours to palliate conduct that ought to excite abhorrence in every virtuous breast" (October 1791, p. 218). *Tristam Shandy*, which was morally suspect in America during much of the eighteenth century, snared the budding author in obscenities as well as misplaced sympathies. In rejecting "A Shandean Fragment", the editors admitted that it was "a tolerable *imitation* of Sterne's manner; but it is too *indelicate*. It is to be regretted that *talents* are not always accompanied by a *judicious taste*. Should our Correspondent continue to exercise his *imitative* faculty, we hope he will hereafter study the *beauties*, not the *imperfections*, of authors" (December 1790, p. 354).

The editors cast the novel into the ninth circle of literary hell. Although Blair had conceded that novels "might be employed for very useful purposes" by furnishing "one of the best channels for conveying instruction, for painting human life and manners, for showing the errors into which we are betrayed by our passions, for rendering virtue amiable and vice odious",[9] the editors of the

9 *Lectures*, II, 196.

Columbian believed that the more usual effect was to render virtue odious and vice irresistible. Fiction did appear in the magazine; but it was seldom praised in the reviews. Such works as John Shippen's pamphlet "Observations on Novel-Reading", which revealed the insidious effect of novels on the young, were recommended enthusiastically "to those parents, and instructors of youth, who have not sufficiently reflected on the pernicious consequences of permitting young minds to imbibe the principles contained in most of our modern novels" (October 1792, p. 262). The magazine printed a lengthy excerpt from Shippen's pamphlet to support its opinion of the morality of novels:

Novels not only pollute the imaginations of young women, but also give them false ideas of life, which too often make them act improperly, owing to the romantic turn of thinking they imbibe from their favorite studies. They read of characters which never existed, and never can exist; and when all the wit and invention of a luxuriant fancy are stretched, to paint a young man all perfection in body and mind, it is hardly possible for a girl to avoid falling in love with the phantom, and being out of humor with the piece of plain mortality which she afterwards marries. . . .

These authors of novels take great pleasure in making their characters act beyond nature. . . . By reading these books, therefore, young people are taught arts which they never could have dreamed of, and their minds being thus led into a wrong train of thinking, it is no wonder that their maturer age is bent on the pursuit of trifles, if not on vicious indulgences.

To illustrate the point that the false impressions of life found in novels could cause a girl to go astray, the "Intelligence" section of the magazine printed sensational cases from real life. In the September 1788 *Columbian* the "Intelligence" told its readers of "An affecting instance of suicide" on the part of a girl of twenty-two "of a genteel family, and a *great reader* of ROMANCES" who took arsenic after "a course of criminal intimacy with a *brother-in-law*, and severe treatment from a *parent*. . . ." According to the magazine, "every step . . . [was] conducted with deliberation, and in the true stile of romance, upon which the mind and manners of this heroine was formed" (p. 541). The most-often quoted testimony against the novel in late eighteenth-century America was the celebrated case of Elizabeth Whitman, which provided the source for Hannah Foster's *The Coquette* and an *exemplum* for numerous sermons, poems, and novels, among them William Hill Brown's *The Power of Sympathy*. The *Columbian* printed the account of Elizabeth Whitman's death during childbirth in a Danvers, Connecticut, tavern in the first issue after the story broke in the Boston papers in August 1788. The editors were quick to connect her fate to novel reading:

It has since been discovered that she was an unmarried lady of reputable family in Connecticut. In her younger days she was admired for her beauty, good sense, and engaging qualities. She was a *great reader of romances*, and having formed her notions of happiness, from that corrupt source, became vain and coquettish, and rejected some very advantageous offers of marriage in hope of realizing something more splendid; till disappointed and past her bloom, she gave way to criminal indulgence, and the consequence becoming visible, she eloped from her friends and terminated her career... (August 1788, p. 473).[10]

Not only did novels create a false impression of life in the young mind, they took American youth away from more useful pursuits. Shippen's pamphlet suggested that rather than read novels young ladies should improve their minds by more proper books, an attitude endorsed by his *Columbian* reviewer, who suggested that "such of our fair readers as inconsiderately trifle away the precious hours of youth in the indiscriminate perusal of novels, will find in the following extracts, some incentives to devote their attention to more useful studies". A review of Reverend Enos Hitchcock's educational novel *Memoirs of the Bloomsgrove Family* not only condemned novels for creating false taste in the young but praised Mr. Bloomsgrove's library because it contained instead of fiction "the writings of the best poets, historians, travels, characters, geography, elements of natural philosophy, and books

---

[10]   This passage appears almost verbatim in William Hill Brown, *The Power of Sympathy* (Boston, 1789), I, 50. Both the *Columbian* and Brown probably copied it from a third source, most likely a Boston newspaper account.

of taste and elegance, miscellaneous, moral, and entertaining"
(September 1790, p. 179). Benjamin Rush condemned novels on
nationalistic grounds. In discussing the education proper for
American youth, he expressed the belief that nothing contained in
novels was useful to life in the new nation since none of the social
refinements they described were practical in the democratic and
primitive society of the United States (April 1790, p. 212).

Nor was the *Columbian* duped by the contention that novels
are useful because they soften the sensibilities. Shippen believed
that "good sentiments being found scattered in loose novels,
render them the more dangerous, since, when they are mixed with
seducing arguments, it requires more discernment than is to be
found in youth to separate the evil from the good" (October 1792,
pp. 225-226). Rush doubted that sentiments in novels have a
genuine effect on the emotions of their readers. "We sometimes
see", he wrote, "instances of young ladies who weep away a
whole forenoon over the criminal sorrows of a fictitious Charlotte
or Werter [sic], turning with disdain at two o'clock from the sight
of a begger" (April 1790, p. 212). Deborah Senrich, in a letter to
Elizabeth Graeme Fergusson, conceded that "our sex is much and
tenderly indebted to the great novelist *Richardson*"; but at the
same time she feared that "the frequent perusal of such delicate,
pathetic, high wrought strokes of superior virtue" as found in his
novels stimulated the sensibility to the point "as to give the attentive reader a disrelish for the more common enjoyments of life"
and "to sharpen the thorns and roughen the rugged paths of life"
to an undesirable degree. She concluded that it was better to
avoid novels and to have a mind "only filled with the common
opinions of *happiness* and *mediocrity* . . ." (March 1791, p. 141).

This censure of the novel resulted partially from the editors'
didacticism and partially from the philosophical objections to
fiction voiced by Scotch common sense realism. The Scotch
philosophers dichotomized life into the actual and the possible.
The actual they defined as possessing physical being perceptible
to the primary senses. The possible, they said, exists in the
intellect and lacks concrete sensory being. Only the actual possesses the sensuous immediacy necessary to form deep and lasting

influences on human character; the effect of the possible is weak and temporary, the difference being like the idea of pain contrasted to an aching tooth. Because fiction relates the possible and not the actual, critics oriented to the Scotch position dismissed it as inferior to the writing of history or biography, which recites the actual.[11]

Furthermore, the Scotch critics believed the actual regulates the imagination and prevents it from exceeding the boundaries of reality. The novel frees the imagination from the restrictions of the actual and makes it liable to create vicious lies. The influence of this critical argument in America, added to the traditional Puritan distrust of fiction expressed in such works as Cotton Mather's *Manuductio ad Ministerium*, formed a critical bulwark against the novel and the romance.[12]

Other genres escaped blanket condemnation; but the editors insisted on a high moral tone from all. The satirist "who attacks foibles, or innocent fashions, with weapons from which decency shrinks, ought to ask himself – which is most likely to prove injurious to society? his indecent satire, or its weak but harmless object . . .?" (June 1792, p. 338). The biographer was urged to exhibit the "republican virtue" of his subject, and the historian to trace the patterns of national virtue in the events of history. Whatever his genre, the strength of an author's moral lesson was the most persuasive argument he could offer for publication.

In demanding universality, the editors departed from the conventional neoclassical practice and defined the universal as the absence of personal or temporary reference rather than as those irreducible principles observable in nature. They believed that in a time of political crisis they must avoid any piece which exhibited a recognizable local personality and which might be construed as politically controversial. Spotswood's experience

---

[11]   Terence Martin, *The Instructed Vision: Scottish Common Sense Philosophy and the Origins of American Fiction* (Bloomington, Ind., 1961), 57-103 treats in detail the Scotch case against fiction.
[12]   The *Columbian* critics accepted this viewpoint and condemned all novels except *The Memoirs of the Bloomsgrove Family*, the high morality of which overcame the reviewer's metaphysical objections to its being fictional.

with the Federalist faction had demonstrated the wisdom of such a policy. The editors received many requests that they print political articles,[13] but they refused on the grounds that every political piece would be considered as a sign of partiality, "either *entirely* on the one side, or *entirely* on the other" (May 1788, p. 236).

In a time when political factiousness was the favorite parlor sport of most American intellectuals, the avoidance of personality and of specific issues seriously limited the editors' quest for lively material. More than once they were forced to make such comments as:

We believe the *Portrait of Frivolus* to be a very just one; but, as every reader in Philadelphia would be able to point out the *original*, we cannot insert it. It has been justly observed, that "public shame amends not the human heart"; if therefore, our correspondent had been actuated by laudable motives, he would have spared the *man* while he exposed the *vice*. (November 1790, p. 282)

In other cases the editors offered to print pieces after they had been purged of personal allusion.[14]

They also rejected articles containing particular references to the affairs of the times or to matters of local interest. The editors told the author of an essay on the establishment of a standing army in the United States that his piece "contains too many remarks of a *temporary* nature. Should he think proper to omit these, we shall chearfully publish that part of his essay which relates to the general subject" (January 1791, p. 2). In reviewing the posthumous publication of Francis Hopkinson's *Essays,* the magazine confidently believed that "had he lived to superintend the publication of them himself, we think it probable that he would either have revised or expunged some of them, which were written to answer purposes of a temporary nature; and others, in which particular characters are severely satirized" (August 1792, p. 111). His failure to do so "cast a shadow" over his work.

---

[13] Among them was a letter from Jeremy Belknap. See the "Belknap Papers", 6th Ser., IV, 409.

[14] See, for example, the "Notes to Contributors" in February 1789, 80, June 1789, 296, and April 1790, 202.

The editors' distaste for the personal also excluded the expression of personal emotion. Although the growing romantic mood sanctioned individual feeling as the artist's proper subject, the *Columbian* clung tenaciously to the principle that emotion was a valid literary subject only when it agreed with the universal emotional sense of mankind. To one enthusiastic poet the editors retorted: "If *Croydon* really does 'With falling tears' his 'charmer's loss deplore', we sincerely pity him; but we cannot perceive what business the public have with an account of his private distress" (February 1791, p. 66). Instead, they urged their contributors to strive for the most universal of all emotions, the sublime. Rather than parade their personal feelings before the reading public, writers were ordered to "inspire the mind with grand and elevated ideas" by describing the vast, the ethereal, and the magnanimous in man and nature, thus raising the mind "considerably above its ordinary pitch".[15] To become personal was to reduce the scale of the image and to destroy the sublime effect.

The definition of the universal as being void to specific reference and the connection of generality with sublimity accounts for much that is bad in the literature which the *Columbian* printed and for the inconsistency in its demand for a national literature. Truly American life was specific, local, and even provincial. The uncouth backwoodsman who emerged in frontier humor, in the national mythology, and in the native tradition of the novel as a unique American literary figure was barred from entry to the magazine by the dictate of universality.[16] Political opinion, which

---

[15]   Compare the *Columbian* statement of June 1792, 338 to Blair, *Lectures*, I, 47. The idea of the sublime found in the *Columbian* was probably derived from Blair rather than from Burke, for it agrees with Blair in those points in which he agrees with Longinus, but not with Burke. See Walter John Hipple, Jr., *The Beautiful, The Sublime, and The Picturesque in Eighteenth-Century British Aesthetic Theory* (Carbondale, Ill., 1957), 122-132 for a full account of the origins of Blair's thought about the sublime, the beautiful, and the picturesque.

[16]   The emergence of the frontiersman in the fiction of James Fenimore Cooper, William Gilmore Simms, Timothy Flint, James Hall, Robert Montgomery Bird and others and in the oral and written traditions of native American humor is too familiar to need documentation. Daniel Hoffman has said that the clash between the Yankee and the backwoodsman became "a major theme in our literature, as well as a continuing

James Fenimore Cooper later called the only valid criterion for distinguishing American from English literature,[17] was likewise prohibited. Subliminity more often than not meant vague diction and pompous rhetoric. Such attitudes retarded the development of a national literature and damaged the quality of the magazine as severely as any other factor in the culture of the time.

Almost as important as universality to the editors was the concept of decorum, which they apparently knew chiefly through Pope's "Essay on Criticism". The favorite comment rejecting a piece for its lack of decorum was to quote Pope's admonition, "Keep probability in view". Fiction seemed, again, particularly liable to criticism. Stories were rejected as "forced and unnatural" and for bordering "too much on the marvellous". In most cases the editors blamed the author's depending upon imagination rather than upon the rational imitation of nature. They protested that "the *singular* character drawn" by one contributor was "the offspring of his own imagination . . .", for "such a compound of contradictions and absurdities is surely not in nature" (August 1792, p. 74).

The *Columbian* related the demand for American subject matter to the sense of decorum rather than to any nascent romanticism. The editors anticipated by almost forty years William Cullen Bryant's criticism of American poems which contained European nightingales. Decorum demanded that American literature be faithful to American manners and landscapes. The editors rejected "Summer, a poem" as "certainly not written in the warm weather of an American summer". "Lucenda, a novel" was unacceptable because "the characters are far too romantic, for the age and country in which we live". "Observator's Strictures on the prevalent vices and follies of the Age" discussed vices which

---

motif in a century and a half of folktales, and in our national history". *Form and Fable in American Fiction* (New York, Oxford University Press, 1965), 84. The proscription against such characters by the editors of the *Columbian* in effect shut the pages of the magazine to the material which was to produce in thirty years the most vital American literature.

[17] *Notions of the Americans*, quoted from *James Fenimore Cooper: Representative Selections*, ed. Robert E. Spiller (New York, American Book Co., 1936), 9.

the editors felt were not common among Americans and which called to the attention of the young harmful follies foreign to American manners. They suggested that "If *Observator* allows such parts of his stricture as are not deemed applicable to American manners, to be expunged, the remainder will be cheerfully inserted" (September 1791, p. 146).

The editors apparently felt that too many of their contributors failed to observe the decorum of American reality. They complained:

We have frequently been obliged to reject well-written performances, because they did not apply to the state of things in this country. Our poetical correspondents often introduce into their rural strains, trees, birds, etc., that are not known in America; and writers on manners and morals are often ridiculous, in consequence of taking their information on these subjects from other countries. (September 1791, p. 146)

The editors blamed this lack of decorum on the fact that American taste was formed by reading and imitating European books rather than by observing American nature, a paradoxical attitude considering that they also advocated imitating the style of European authors. The editors commented that "there are two kinds of imagination, one is acquired by an early intimacy with the magnificent scenes of nature, the other is taken, at second hand, from books". Thus, they reasoned, the American poet who imitates his European counterpart is liable to include "larks, linnets, nightingales, cookoos, ravens, jackadaws, . . . magpies" and other images not native to America. Considering that he was simultaneously urged to imitate the style in which the European poet used these tabooed images, there is little wonder that the American poet was confused about the proper role of imitation in literature and that the quality of his work reflects that confusion.

Decorum of language and tone applied to style just as decorum of probability did to action and character. On numerous occasions the editors reminded their contributors that "there is a certain necessary relation between the style and the subject of the composition. . . ." They opposed equally the use of colloquialism for "elevated" themes and the presentation of "trifling and low subjects . . . in all the *energy of diction* and *rotundity of periods* of the Rambler" (August 1791, p. 74). "A poetical address from Horatio to the sacred object of his affections" was written in "the doggrel or burlesque manner" unsuited to a love poem (October 1792, p. 218). An Oriental tale was rejected because "the Eastern stile is not supported throughout" (May 1787, p. 400).

The "Impartial Review" applied the same principles to the works it considered. A reviewer attacked Mrs. Sarah Wentworth Morton's poem *Ouabi: Or the Virtues of Nature* not only because of its romantic characterization of the American Indian but because it used "the awkward measure which has long been appropriated to elegies" and because the poet did not change her meter for passages of dialogue. He expressed the opinion that English heroic measure was infinitely better suited to her subject (February 1791, p. 107). The reviewer of an anonymous poem entitled "To the Enslaved Africans, *in the character of an ancient* Negro, *born a slave in* Pennsylvania; *but liberated some years since, and instructed in useful learning and the great truths of Christianity*" found the style too languid for a poem dealing with the evils of slavery, a subject which seemed to call for more spirit. But he was not disturbed by the fact that the old Negro spoke in correct English couplets (December 1790, p. 403).

The magazine's comments on style involved standards of correctness and elegance based on the authoritarian grammar and rhetoric of late-eighteenth-century England. The "Notes to Contributors" abounds with such statements as "The Elegiac Verses to the memory of T. J. are too incorrect for public view", "the author's intention appears to be laudable, but . . . the language [is] incorrect", "To - - - - on the death of their son, is replete with good sentiments; but as a poem it is not sufficiently correct and finished . . . the public eye will make no allowances", and "we are sorry *The Muse of America* proves too incorrect for publication".[18] Scarcely a book escaped the stigma of linguistic and stylistic incorrectness. The reviewer of William Bartram's *Travels* praised the book for its "useful information and agreeable

---

[18] *Columbian*, May 1787, 400; January 1788, 2; January 1789, 2; and June 1791, 362.

entertainment . . .", but refused to "countenance a style so very incorrect and disgustingly pompous, as that in which the greater part of these travels is written" (April 1792, p. 267). Of Hugh Henry Brackenridge's *Modern Chivalry* the reviewer stated: "Mr. B. affects to write merely for the sake of style, but no person, who has perused the work, can, for a moment, look upon this pretension in a serious light" (August 1792, p. 116). The best most authors could hope from the *Columbian* was that it would recommend their work in spite of its style. Few escaped its wish that "our author had endeavoured to write more correctly. . . ." (March 1791, p. 183).

The *Columbian's* standard of correctness had a twin basis. Negatively, it looked to grammars like Robert Baker's *Remarks on the English Language* and Robert Lowth's *Short Introduction* for proscriptions of usages considered incorrect, illogical, or "barbarous".[19] Positively, it sought a standard for elegant expression in the rhetorics of Hugh Blair and Lord Kames and in the examples of Swift, Addison, and Johnson. Working between these two poles, it formed a narrowly mechanical academic conception of good language and style.

A dispute with Noah Webster clearly defined the issue of correctness. In October and November 1790 the "Impartial Review" bitterly attacked Webster's *Fugitiv Essays*. After ridiculing Webster's qualifications as a linguist, the reviewer listed forty specific violations of correctness in the author's own style. Webster replied with a long letter which appeared in September and October 1791. He answered the forty points one by one, admitting that some were his mistakes, calling others typographical errors, and challenging the reviewer's condemnation of the rest. The *Columbian* replied to Webster's letter at the end of the October issue.

This exchange marks, as far as I have been able to ascertain, the first public debate in America between the authoritarian and

---

[19]   The doctrine of linguistic correctness in eighteenth-century England is traced in Sterling A. Leonard, *The Doctrine of Correctness in English Usage 1700-1800*, University of Wisconsin Studies in Language and Literature, No. 25 (Madison, 1929).

the descriptive approaches to grammar.[20] The lines are clearly drawn: the *Columbian* favors the authority of Lowth, Baker, and their academic followers; Webster asserts the linguist's role as describer, not legislator, of language. The crux is the role of education in forming style.

Earlier the *Columbian* had blamed the incorrectness of American style on "the want of a due attention to our native language ... in the system of education established in most of our seminaries of learning" (May 1791, p. 336). Webster attacked this academic bias and the critic who accepts it:

He must be some person who has lately left a grammar school, who has learnt to speak by *square* and *compass,* who supposes the language to be made by *grammar rules,* and not those rules by settled practice, and thus believes every expression for which he has no grammar rule, is not good English. I am not surprised to find him thus fettered by arbitrary rules. Our Colleges are in the same situation, and so are most of the public seminaries in Great Britain. I was in the same situation myself, while my enquiries respecting language were confined to dictionaries and grammars. I finally deserted them, and attempted to examine the authorities on which Johnson, Lowth, and other compilers have built their opinions. The result was, that I found incontestible evidence to overthrow one half of the rules of the English grammars now in use; and a multitude of phrases of good English, for which these grammars give us *no rules at all.* The phrases, *then* is the *time, now* is the *time,* come within the last mentioned description. They are as correct phrases as any in the language. To satisfy a little pedantic critic of the propriety of them, the phrases might be altered thus, *the time is now,* or *was then;* for *now* and *then* are in sense mere abreviations of the *present* time *or past time.* But to a man who is not fettered by rules, in cases where rules are imperfect, or arbitrary, the phrases appear vindicable on the ground of *settled, general, immemorial practice,* the *only* ground on which *all* grammars must stand, if they have any support but private opinion. (October 1791, p. 260)

Webster also accused Lowth and the others of introducing "some

---

[20]   John Witherspoon discussed vulgarisms, Americanisms, and local dialects in "The Druid", *Pennsylvania Journal*, May 1781; but he did not become involved in a theoretical discussion of the conflicts between descriptive and proscriptive grammar. His papers are reprinted in *The Beginnings of American English*, ed. M. M. Mathews (Chicago, 1931), 13-43.

innovations which *corrupt the purity* of our language." His own purpose, he asserted, was to discountenance the innovations of authoritarian grammarians and "to bring back the language to its *former purity. ...*" (*ibid.*, p. 264).

The editors refused to retract a word of their review and, in their "Remarks on Mr. Webster's letter", reasserted their belief in the authority of English grammarians:

Mr. Webster, in his defence of the stile of his essays, discovers an extraordinary degree of obstinacy, if not of ignorance of the principles and genius of the English language. ... *his assertion* cannot be considered as authority sufficient to give currency to phrases, which almost every *school-boy* knows to be incorrect; that a peculiar practice in Connecticut, or even in the whole of N. England, is not sufficient to justify his use of the word *conduct*, etc. ... As for grammar rules, unless they are of his own forming, it would very much curb his genius to pay any attention to them. We hope, therefore, he will continue to treat the whole tribe of English grammarians and lexicographers with the contempt of a man who is conscious of his own superiority. But, above all, if he wishes to perfect his stile, upon the plan he has so well begun, he must studiously avoid even the most distant attention to the writings of Swift, Bolingbroke, Addison, or any of those English authors whose stile is admired by us reviewers, and by such other vulgar judges as know no better. (October 1791, p. 266)

This statement contains the essence of the magazine's views on style: the rules must be followed; the best models must be imitated; romantic irregularity must not be tolerated. English authority outweighed American practice.

Most of the specific instances of Webster's incorrectness cited by the reviewer are violations of logic. Reason formed one of the cornerstones of authoritative grammar. Hugh Blair's lectures XX through XXIV gave a detailed *explication de texte* of the styles of Addison, Swift, and Steele; his most frequent criticism was the illogical use of words. For example, of Addison's phrase "*extension, shape, and all other ideas that enter at the eye. ...*" Blair said: "*Extension and shape* can, with no propriety, be called *ideas*; they are properties of matter".[21] Such careful, if not per-

[21]   *Lectures*, I, 291.

nickety, application of logic set the precedent for the *Columbian* reviewer's questioning the logic of Webster's phrases *undisguised frankness* (how can an abstraction wear a disguise?), *value is appraised* (what is appraisal but the ascertaining of value?), *his standing in life* (how can an abstraction stand?), and *venture an opinion* (how does the expression of opinion qualify as adventurous?). Webster defended these phrases by asserting that their logicality was a matter of personal opinion, and his opinion was that they were correct.

The reviewer attacked other of Webster's usages on the grounds of their "barbarism", which meant either that he had coined a word or that he was using one part of speech as another.[22] Webster defended his use of the word *happified* on the grounds that it was a common usage in Connecticut (the OED records the first appearance of the word in 1612 and cites a use of it in a New England collection of poems in 1786). The phrase *schoolmate attachment*, Webster said, was quoted from a letter written to him by a New England woman and thus reflected normal usage in that area. But the editors rejected this explanation, saying that ignorant usage was no justification for incorrectness.

Most of the other contested usages involved the logic of prepositions. Webster defended a number of these by citing equivalent usages in respected English authors of the century. But the editors were not impressed.

Not all reactions to style in the *Columbian* were negative. Books were praised stylistically for two apparent reasons: either the author was connected with the publishers of the magazine or his style satisfied their rather mechanical standard of excellence, which was based on rhetorical shibboleths. The "Impartial Review" lavishly admired Benjamin Rush, whose connection with the magazine as paid contributor was perhaps not irrelevant to the praise. South Carolina historian David Ramsay received the

---

[22] Leonard, p. 66 points out that "It was generally understood in the eighteenth-century grammars that the same word may appear as more than one part of speech, ... But the feeling that there should be differences in terminations for the various parts of speech led to careful scrutiny of all cases. ... "

editors' highest encomiums, for not only was he writing with a nationalistic purpose but he also had close personal connections in Philadelphia. The Reverend William Smith was Provost of the Academy of Philadelphia, a close friend of the publishers and editors, eulogist of Benjamin Franklin, and an acclaimed patriotic orator; he was, therefore, above criticism. Such qualifications transcended even a knowledge of Blair's *Rhetoric*; when combined with a careful imitation of the doctrines of linguistic and rhetorical correctness, they provided an excellence which the editors were ready to match against the finest England could offer.

The most common terms of praise used by the editors and reviewers do little to clarify their stylistic ideals: authors are "pure, dignified, and correct", "simple and elegant" and possess "vigorous imagination, grandeur of thought, energy of style, and warm benevolence of sentiment". Rush is praised for "the beautiful ease and simplicity in style, the correct language, the bold expressive metaphors, the judicious observations, and the exalted sentiments, which characterize this elegant performance" (August 1790, p. 110). Strength and beauty of metaphor always elicited praise. The following example from Benjamin Rush's "Eulogium in honour of the late Dr. William Cullen" satisfied rhetorical requirements for metaphor such as Blair's seven rules in the Lecture XV: "His mind had no rubbish in it. Like a secretory organ, in the animal body, it rejected every thing in reading, that could not be applied in some useful purpose" (August 1790, p. 111). The reviewer found the metaphor particularly appropriate to the subject of a deceased physician.[23]

Perhaps the highest praise a reviewer or an editor could accord an author was that his style was sublime. Although titularly agreeing with Blair that sublimity resides in the object described rather than in the rhetoric of the description,[24] the reviewers

---

[23] See Blair, *Lectures*, I, 208-223 for the rules for metaphor.

[24] Blair wrote: "I distinguish these two things from one another, the Grandeur of the objects themselves when they are presented to the eye, and the description of that Grandeur in discourse or writing ... the Sublime is a species of writing which depends less than any other on the artificial embellishments of rhetoric. ...." *Lectures*, I, 33 and 41.

tended in practice to praise passages of rhetorical density, particularly if devoted to a patriotic subject. Reverend William Smith's "Eulogium on Benjamin Franklin" and "A Sermon on temporal and spiritual salvation" satisfied both the desire for rhetoric and for patriotism. The reviewer quoted two lengthy passages employing personification and apostrophe, two figures which Hugh Blair called the boldest and most sublime of all,[25] and praised them for their grandeur. Like so many passages admired during the post-Revolutionary period, the quotations address the personified United States:

Be wise, then, be instructed, ye rising *American States*! Let it be your glorious contention which of you shall stand foremost in making liberal provisions for the advancement and support of *freedom* and *virtue*; ... by wise establishments for the instruction of youth, the advancement of the arts and sciences, the encouragement of industry, and the maintenance of *religion* and *morality* – this shall become a great and happy land!

Another sublime figure, which Blair called "vision", followed:

Transported at the thought, I am borne forward to days of distant renown! In my expanded view, these *United States* rise, in all their ripened glory, before me. I look, through, and beyond, every yet peopled region of the New World, and behold period still brightening upon period. Where one continuous depth of gloomy wilderness now shuts out even the beams of day, I see new *states* and *empires*, new seats of *wisdom* and *knowledge*, new *religious* domes, spreading around. In places now untrod by any but savage beasts, or men as savage as they, I hear the voice of happy labour, and behold towery cities growing into the skies! (September 1790, p. 177)

Such passages the editors admired because they could be measured mechanically against a dogmatic scale of sublime rhetoric and patriotic sentiment. Metaphors could be counted and judged for appropriateness, apostrophes could be admired, visions of a utopian America could be exulted in.

Such critical ideas as generality and correctness hindered literary nationalism in two ways. First, they excluded from literature uniquely American manners, characters, and language. The

[25] *Lectures*, I, 228-240 discusses personification and apostrophe.

American idiom embodied those elements of national character which distinguished American experience: boisterous humor, restless energy, and intense independence. But the rules of correctness and generality censored those very characteristics which made the American language expressive of national aspirations and achievements. Similarly, the times surged with events which were shaping the destiny of the nation: westward expansion, the political warfare surrounding the constitutional convention, the forging of policies which directed the course of American history for decades to come. But the doctrine of generality forbade the use of such "local and temporary" subjects and doomed writing to a mediocre abstraction.

Secondly, the prevalence of neoclassical ideas in the early national period retarded the birth of the romantic spirit in America. One of the significant effects of Romanticism was to free literary language from the conventional epithets and stock phrases common during the last half of the eighteenth century and to restore the fresh perception of detail to its rightful place as the basis of literary art. America offered the writer a vast field of virgin images in its landscape, its manners, its humor, and its national character. But the rhetorical dogmas of Blair and his American followers forced these images into prearranged categories such as the sublime, the sentimental, the heroic, and the gothic. Critics, editors, and academicians unwittingly locked the American imagination in a British prison.

The critical comments of the *Columbian Magazine* reveal the paradox that while its editors demanded a native American literature, they judged it by standards that made its existence impossible. The effect of this paradox can be seen in the trite and imitative literature which the magazine printed.

III

AMERICAN IDEALS AND BRITISH GENRES

In 1825, William Cullen Bryant, speaking of the poets of the late eighteenth century, bemoaned their enslavement to imitation. "Instead of copying nature with the aid of knowledge derived from these models", he wrote, the poet "has been induced to make them the original, from which the copy was to be drawn. He has been led to take an imperfect work . . . as the standard of perfection, and to dwell upon it with such reverence that he comes to see beauties where no beauties are. . . ." More specifically, he condemned the followers of Pope, noting that Pope himself had learned from the whole range of literary tradition but that they modeled their work on Pope alone and thereby initiated a decline in the art of poetry.[1]

Bryant's criticism applies to all the writers whose work appeared in the *Columbian Magazine* and describes a serious defect of American writing during the early national period. Poets and prose writers alike imitated a small group of eighteenth-century English authors. Fiction copied either Richardson's seduction tale, Sterne's sentimentality, or Goldsmith and Johnson's Oriental tales. The couplet ruled poetry. Although odes, lyrics, and elegies often took mid-century poets Shenstone, Collins, Gray, and Thomson as their models, Pope remained the monitor of taste.[2]

---

[1] "On Originality and Imitation", *Prose Writings of William Cullen Bryant*, ed. Parke Godwin (New York, Russell and Russell, Inc., 1964), I, 40-42.

[2] Fourteen editions of the *Essay on Man* alone appeared in America during the lifetime of the *Columbian*, and Pope's influence extended well into the next century. Samuel Knapp, *American Cultural History 1607-1826* (Gainesville, Fla., 1961), 186, expressed a preference for Pope over the

Periodical essays unimaginatively copied the *Spectator, Tatler, Rambler*, and their poorer followers. In genre as well as in theory, American literature was chained to England.

One cause of the lack of originality might have been a corruption of the neoclassical theory of genre. According to the neoclassic critics, imitating other authors, preferably the classics, gave the poet an established formal pattern within which to structure his own images and ideas. Dryden, in his "Preface to the Translation of Ovid's Epistles", asserted the imitator's "liberty, not only to vary from the words and sense, but to forsake them both as he sees occasion; and ... [take] only some general hints from the original. ..." [3] These hints were both structural and verbal. For example, not only did the form of the Horation Ode help the poet organize his own view of nature into lines and stanzas, Horace's images, diction, and rhythms stimulated his imagination to further insights and images. But, by the late eighteenth century, the idea of imitation had broadened into an acceptance of the imitated work's verbal patterns as well as its form. Not only Pope's couplet, but his diction, his syntax, his images, and his ideas became sacred objects. American writers, following the British example, borrowed the content as well as the form of English poetry and, in so doing, undermined the ideal of American literary independence.

The literature in the *Columbian* would have been as much at home in London as in Philadelphia. Poetry, fiction, and periodical essays slavishly copied English works. Biography, history, and geographical and topographical descriptions showed more independence but still followed the style and organization of their English counterparts. What American originality did exist was stifled by the rigidity of the imitation of British models.

Except for occasional adumbrations of romantic verse, neoclassical forms dominated the "Columbian Parnassiad". Four types composed approximately eighty percent of the poetry in

---

Romantic poets as late as 1826. For the popularity of Pope during the early national period see Agnes Marie Sibley, *Alexander Pope's Prestige in America 1725-1835* (New York, 1949).

[3] *Essays of John Dryden*, ed. W. P. Ker (Oxford, 1900), I, 237.

the magazine: odes and ode-like occasional verse, *vers de société*, elegies, and didactic and philosophical verse. The remaining twenty percent included satire, beast fables, topographical verse, versifications of Ossian, sonnets, excerpts from epics, and miscellaneous curiosities.

The most ambitious poems in the magazine were odes and occasional poems of the type which Gordon E. Bigelow calls "partisan" and "epideictic".[4] These poems, which constituted approximately twenty-five percent of all poetry in the magazine, were highly rhetorical in structure and diction. The rules set down by Blair for achieving the elevated style dictated most of their effects. For example, Blair remarked that apostrophes to inanimate or personified objects are more sublime than apostrophes to living beings.[5] In response, Ann Young Smith began her "Ode to Liberty"

> Hail Liberty, thou godess bright!
> Grand source of every pure delight
> The virtuous heart desires. . . .
> (February 1791, p. 113)

and David Humphreys addressed the abstract goddess of the new nation: "Then awake, Columbia! daughter of the skies, / Awake to glory and to greatness rise!" (March 1788, p. 165). Other odes employed images of vague and spacious landscape, inverted sentence structure, extended metaphors and conceits, and all the other trappings of the sublime style. Francis Hopkinson even borrowed a vigorous metaphor from Shakespeare to begin his "Ode" written for the Federal Procession of July 4, 1788: "Oh for a muse of fire! to mount the skies / And to a list'ning world proclaim –" (July 1788, p. 409).

Of course, rhetorical organization and style are neither new

---

[4] *Rhetoric and American Poetry of the Early National Period*, University of Florida Monographs, No. 4 (Spring, 1960), 48. Professor Bigelow defines the partisan as "versified propaganda, designed to move a particular group of men to some desired action, to pursuade them to believe in one cause or to reject another . . . " and the epideictic as combining "a dominant purpose of praise or blame, along with highly ornamented, extravagant style".

[5] *Lectures*, I, 238.

nor particularly American. American poets during the Revolution had relied heavily upon rhetorical verse modeled on Dryden and Pope as a political weapon,[6] and the tradition carried over into the spirit of nationalism. Bombastic patriotic cantata odes similar in form and rhetoric to the odes praising George III which filled the pages of *Gentleman's Magazine* became the favorite poetic type of the early national period.[7] Most of them were written to be performed musically on specific occasions. For example, Hopkinson's "Temple of Minerva" was presented in the suite of the French ambassador in February 1781 to celebrate the recent alliance between the United States and France. Titles such as "Ode sung at the Great Wigwam of the Tammany Society ... of New York, on the Celebration of the third Century of the Discovery of America by Columbus", "Ode; on the establishment of Sunday-Schools in Philadelphia", "Ode Sacred to the Arrival of Congress in Philadelphia", "ODE, sacred to the memory of Dr. Franklin ... performed at the Public Commencement, in the College of Philadelphia, July 17, 1790", and "An Ode, on the Birth of the Dauphin of France. Presented to His Excellency, The Chevalier de la Suzeirie, Minister from the King of France, to the United States of America; on the morning of an Entertainment given on that occasion" suggest the particular occasions for which the poems were written.[8]

A number of poems retained the word *ode* in their titles, using it in its original connotation of lyrical composition. Their subjects were usually artificially pastoral. Some, like the "Anacreontic ODE, on the approach of SPRING", nationalized the pastoral imagery of poets like Thomson and Dyer by locating it geographically, if not spiritually, in America; but most addressed the seasons and the sympathetic passions in lofty generalization and vague formulae.

[6]   See Tyler, *Literary History of the American Revolution*, I, 22; and Elder Olsen, "Rhetoric and the Appreciation of Pope", *Modern Philology*, XXXVII (1939), 13-35.
[7]   For a discussion of the cantata ode in English see George N. Shuster, *The English Ode from Milton to Keats* (New York, 1940), 170-178.
[8]   For these poems see the *Columbian*, February 1787, 295; April 1787, 391; November 1790, 339; February 1791, 116; and October 1792, 264.

The most frequently used form was tetrameter couplets. The Horatian pattern of a repeated stanza form was also common, usually with tetrameter quatrains, a six-line tetrameter stanza rimed *ababcc*, or "Short Measure" hymn stanza. The Cowleyan pseudo-Pindaric Ode with irregular stanzas appeared rarely, and when it was used, less relationship existed between form and meaning than in Cowley and his eighteenth-century imitators. Even when stanza forms were irregular, they suggest that the poet was combining commonplace stanzas rather than allowing his thought to seek out an original pattern of its own, as illustrated by the following combination of couplets and quatrains from the "Ode Sacred to the arrival of Congress":

> *Americans*! from these, and others learn –
> (Lo! History displays her page)
> Truths, which yourselves or offspring must concern;
> Nor longer in disputes engage.
> Submit in time to just command.
> (See, and revere the illustrious band,
> Who, for your good, in solemn council met,
> Enact new laws, or old repeal;
> Watch faithful o'er the public weal.)
> Union embrace, and former feuds forget.
> (November 1790, p. 339)

Metrically, the rhythms of Pope's couplets and of Watts' hymns dominated. Poets exhibited little subtlety or skill in metrical variation, and what variety did exist can best be characterized as the collapse of form. Even in the cantata odes, musical sense seems almost totally absent.

Rivaling the ode in popularity was a mass of occasional *vers de société* which constituted approximately twenty percent of the poetry in each issue. These short lyrics of between ten and fifty lines imitated the style and subject matter of William Shenstone's lyrics and odes.[9] The poets writing American social verse were,

---

[9] The debt to Shenstone is admitted in John Swanwick's "To Mrs. Howard, on her Marriage" (September 1787, 669), which longs for "Shenstone's lyre, – to sound the verse". In October 1789, 613, two stanzas from Shenstone were printed followed by a Latin translation of one of them by John Carey.

for the most part, amateurs, many of them women, who addressed poems to friends and acquaintances on such occasions as
birthdays, marriages, anniversaries, parties, dances, or merely
Sunday walks.[10] Metrically the poems used quatrains or couplets
of iambic tetrameter, the measures most common in Shenstone.
Simple conceits, rudimentary classical allusions, and commonplace metaphors formed their imagery, and obviousness and
triviality, their most common effect.

Much of the social verse in the *Columbian* was so personal
in allusion as to be almost incomprehensible to the reader not
familiar with the social milieu from which it sprang. Although it
is possible to determine that a lyric in praise of Faelex Brunot is
addressed to a popular Philadelphia hairdresser and that "To
Miss Peggy Chew, with a bow of ribbons found after a dance"
and its companion piece "To Mrs. Howard, on her Marriage" [11]
both refer to the celebrated Philadelphia beauty, Peggy Chew,
who married a descendant of Henry Howard, Earl of Surrey,
extensive identification of personal allusions would be of little
value. Few of these poems have even the mechanical inventive-
ness of Ann Young Smith's "Epistle from Sylvia to Damon;
accompanied with a small writing desk, containing a letter case
and broken mirror, which the author had received, when very
young, as a premium for her proficiency in writing", which
turned the desk and its contents into a conceit expressing the
poet's love for her husband.

Elegies for public figures such as Francis Hopkinson, Benjamin
Franklin, Governor Livingston, and General Warren were
epideictic and eulogistic in tone. Written exclusively in iambic
tetrameter and pentameter couplets, they celebrated the accomplishments of the dead hero and compared him to the greats of

---

[10]   See, for example, Swanwick's "Walk through State House Yard"
(August 1787, 609-610).
[11]   These poems appeared in June 1787, 505 and September 1787, 669.
"Washington's Household Account Book, 1793-1797", *Pennsylvania Maga-
zine of History and Biography*, XXX (1906), 163, records a payment to
Brunot for dressing Mrs. Washington's hair. Miss Chew receives promi-
nent mention in Rufus Wilmot Griswold, *The Republican Court* (New
York, 1855), 339.

the past. Allusions to Roman history suggested a parallel American greatness.[12] The formal progression of the classical elegy from grief to consolation was largely absent, although Ann Young Smith's elegy on General Warren promised that "... future *Warrens* shall protect our land – / A great, united, and illustrious band" (May 1791, p. 341).

The rhetorical enumeration of the public deeds of the hero, particularly those related to American freedom and progress, created a mood less of grief than of triumph that such a man had lived and served in America.

The more personal elegies tended to be pietistic in tone and to offer the conventional Christian consolation that the departed had gone to a better rest. The opening lines of "On hearing the Bell, announcing the Death of Mrs. Margaret Reed" anticipated the sentimentality of nineteenth-century magazine verse:

> Hark! she's gone! that bell proclaims her dead;
> *Reed's* spotless soul, up to her God hath fled.
> Attending angels guard their heav'nly guest,
> Where joys consumate wait her 'mongst the blest. . . .
> (March 1787, p. 344)

Elizabeth Graeme Fergusson, normally a poet of some sensitivity, reverted to the fourteener and commonplace sentiments when addressing consolation to a friend on the death of her son:

> Why does the mother's stricken heart
>   Incessantly repine?
> Why find it still so hard to part,
>   And *innocence* resign?
>
> From sin, from pain, and sorrow torn,
>   An offering due to heaven;

---

[12] Howard Mumford Jones, *O Strange New World*, Chapter VII, treats in considerable detail the influence of American admiration of classical Rome on American place names, literature, and iconography. The agrarian basis of Roman classical hardiness and virtue was paralleled to the agrarian democracy of the new American nation to give evidence of the inevitable rising glory of America. In a later chapter I will discuss the identification of Revolutionary heroes with famous Romans, which was a common rhetorical technique in patriotic poetry, sermons, and speeches.

> For that blest end the babe was born,
> Just lent but, never given.
>
> (June 1791, p. 410)

The traditional Christian conventions governing consolation apparently ruled out any truly poetic expression, even among the talented.

"Paulus, a Modony" was one of the few imitations of the pastoral elegy. Its young shepherd died before he could accomplish his worldly task of helping America win independence; the consolation was not divine, but political: "Short is the gloomy despot's sway, / But freedom's radiant form shall never know decay" (March 1787, p. 343).

David Humphreys' "Elegy on the Burning of Fairfield" and Ann Young Smith's "Elegy on the American Volunteers" rhetorically aroused the reader's hatred of the British rather than consoled any grief he might have felt over the death of his countrymen. Humphreys characterized the British commander at Fairfield as a sadistic savage and bombarded the reader with bloody images of the suffering of the town's citizens:

> See age and sickness, tremulously slow,
> Creep from the flames – see babes in torture die –
> And mothers swoon in agonies of woe.
> Go, gaze, enraptur'd with the virgin's tear,
> The infant's terror, and the captive's pain. . . .
>
> (October 1786, p. 94)

Mrs. Smith ended her sentimental evocation of "the widow's heart-felt anguish" and "the orphan's tear" with a consolation borrowed from Pope – *"Whatever is, is best"* (May 1791, pp. 186-87). Although called elegies, these poems bear more resemblance to the magazine's odes and occasional poems than to elegiac verse.

The didactic poetry in the magazine was written for specific situations and for the purpose of instructing its readers in general and universal principles of morality. In both thought and form it imitated Pope. Such poems as "The vanity of being dissatisfied over our Situation" and "A Sentiment" repeated the philosophical and moral principles of the *Essay on Man* and often quoted Pope as a climactic authority:

> Dull sighted mortals puff'd with pride
>   From truth's just mirror turn their sight,
> In errors wade without a guide,
>   To lead them to the fount of light.
>
> Let them with mad'ning passions rage,
>   And grope about in endless night;
> No more with fate a war I'll wage,
>   But yield convinc'd whatever is – is right.
>
> (July 1789, p. 436)

A favorite subject for moralizing was slavery, a fact reflecting the strong Quaker influence in Philadelphia. "The Dying Slave", "The Dying Negro", "Thomas and Hons", and "The Slave" appeal to the reader's sensibility by describing the misery of the living and the magnanimity of the dying slave. Some end with praise for Benezet and Pennsylvania Quakers, and most use all the devices of rhetoric to touch the emotions of the reader.

The influence of the Graveyard School is perceptible in such poems as "Verses on the Mystery of Man", "Thoughts on Life, Death, and Immortality", and "Colon and Lucy". In the latter, Lucy visits Colon's grave and talks with his ashes, which rise from the ground. They tell her of the horrors of the grave and the vanity of human wishes and sink back into the earth, leaving her to die on his tombstone. Other poems compared the transitoriness of earthly life to the eternal happiness of heaven and recommended that the reader forsake earthly vanity and look to the afterlife. Images of corruption and death enforced the didactic message, and the ghost of Robert Blair hovered overhead.

Two didactic poems adumbrated the American Dream, although stylistically they imitated the verbal patterns of Pope. "The Farmer" recommended American agrarian life as the most virtuous and satisfying existence on earth. "Moral Influenza" attacked the corrupt morals of Europe and suggested that America gave mankind a last opportunity for moral greatness. The presence of both the agrarian and the Adamic themes reveals the long continuity behind their emergence in the literature of the American renaissance fifty years later.[13]

Since the editorial policy forbade political and religious controversy, satire played a minor role in the "Parnassiad". From the Connecticut Wits the editors borrowed poems attacking political situations outside Philadelphia. Lemuel Hopkins' "Apostate Apostle" assaults Ethen Allen with personal invective, but his "Hypocrite's Hope" handles Shays' Rebellion more delicately. A few anonymous poets imitated Pope's moral epistles, satirizing a specific character type such as "The Old Maid" or "The Fashionable Lady". One inspired patriot parodied Hamlet's "To be, or not to be" with "To part, or not to part", but independence was scarcely a dangerous topic in 1788. "The African Lodge", which claimed to be an oration delivered before the first lodge of Negro Masons in America,[14] inverted the arguments of Negro mental and cultural inferiority to support their claim as being the original Masons. Frequent refrains of "pass the jug" and the humorous description of the brothers' reaction prevented the poem from becoming propagandistic. Generally, however, the magazine's satire flayed a harmless object with dull invective.

Satiric beast fables thrived during the first two years of the magazine's life but declined sharply after December 1788. Four of these fables have obvious political overtones. Hopkinson's "The Birds, the Beasts, and the Bat" (March 1787), written in 1778, satirized those Philadelphians who turned coats during the

---

[13]   These themes are treated in considerable detail in Henry Nash Smith, *The Virgin Land* (New York, 1950); R. W. B. Lewis, *The American Adam* (Chicago, 1955); Leo Marx, *The Machine in the Garden* (New York, Oxford University Press, 1964); and Howard Mumford Jones, *O Strange New World*. Jones points out that the roots of the idea of agrarian America as a new garden of Eden sink deep into the soil of medieval and Renaissance Europe. Most of the images and ideas contained in the myth were present in classical antiquity. Modified by the collapse of the medieval world order and by the discovery of the new continent, they took the shape which still later became a national myth.

[14]   The poem parodies a speech made by prominent Boston Negro Prince Hall to the Charlestown, Mass., lodge of Negro Masons in June, 1792. Hall's speech was printed later in the summer by Thomas and John Fleet in Boston and would have been known by the anonymous author of the *Columbian* parody.

Revolution in response to whichever side occupied the city. It described a war between the birds and beasts in which the bat claimed to belong to whichever side was winning and ended ostracized by both. "The Attorney, the Physician, and the Snow Bird" (October 1787) referred obscurely to Shays' Rebellion, and "The Republic of Beasts" (November 1787) and "Political Fox-craft" (September 1788) satirized the difficulties of achieving a stable American government.

Other beast fables satirized society: "The Transformation" (July 1788) described a monkey who turned into a beau; "The Wolf and the Carved Head" (November 1787) depicted a wolf who loved a beautiful painted head but came to his senses when he learned that it had no brains. Peter Markoe's "The Black Bird's Nest" (September 1787) concerned a lustful priest, and "The China Cup and the Pennsylvania Jug" (April 1791) contrasted the strength of plainness and virtue to the weakness of beauty and vanity. Although these fables represent a small percentage of the poetry in the "Parnassiad", they were written with wit and taste and provided a pleasant diversion from the heavier odes, elegies, and didactic verses.

The remaining poetry in the "Parnassiad" was distributed among a number of other types. The desire for a national epic paralleling Virgil's was satisfied by the publication of two long excerpts from Joel Barlow's recently published *Vision of Columbus*. After printing in May 1787 Columbus's vision of America's future greatness and the men who would be its heroes, the editors commented that "this poem, written with true poetic energy, and enrich'd with a great variety of just and elegant sentiments, does honor to the author and to his country". Another form of epic appeared in eleven "translations from Ossian". The first American imitation of Ossian appeared in the *Columbian* in 1786,[15] and a number of imitators, among them Joseph Brown Ladd, continued their publication through January 1791, after which the vogue apparently declined. Most of these imitations "versified" Ossian into polished neoclassical couplets, in spite of the editors' sugges-

---

[15] Frederic I. Carpenter, "The Vogue of Ossian in America", *American Literature*, II (1931), 409.

tion in April 1790 that the heroic couplet was ill suited to "the expressive conciseness of Ossian" because it forced the poet "either to extend a sentiment to two lines, or frequently to conclude a sentence in the middle of a line".

Nascent romanticism is manifest not only in the Ossian but in two versifications of letters from Goethe's *The Sorrows of Werther* which appeared in the September 1787 and January 1791 "Parnassiad". Another efflux of the more sophisticated romanticism of the late eighteenth century was a single Della Cruscan piece in March 1791. Other minor curiosities included three imitations of "Il Penseroso" and one of Milton's nativity ode, all demonstrating an instinct for selecting the worst characteristics of their models to imitate, a translation of a passage from Theocritus in December 1787, one from Boethius in February 1790, and a "Versification" of Chaucer's description of the Parson in the same issue. The first sonnets printed in an American periodical appeared in the "Parnassiad",[16] but they exhibit the editor's desperation for material better than the literary currents of the day. The same can be said of five translations of Biblical passages into neoclassical couplets.

A single piece of American antiquarianism, the first American publication of William Morrell's "New England: Or a Briefe enarration of the ayre, earth, water, fish, and foules of that country", written in the 1620's, deserves mention. Morrell, an Anglican clergyman, came to Weymouth, Massachusetts, in 1623 with Captain Robert Gorges, empowered by the Ecclesiastical Court to govern whatever Anglican churches might be established in that teritory. He remained for a year and inquired into the natural history, geography, and government of the colony. The result was a Latin poem, accompanied by an English translation, which was printed in England in 1625. Jeremy Belknap obtained a copy of the poem and submitted it to the *Columbian*, which printed it in July 1788.[17]

---

[16]   H. Carter Davidson, "The Sonnet in Seven Early American Magazines and Newspapers", *American Literature*, IV (1932), 180-187.
[17]   The poem was later reprinted in the first volume of the *Massachusetts Historical Society Collections* (1792) which mistakenly called that the first

A great deal of the poetry printed in the magazine during its last year appears to have been used as filler. Either original American poems no longer came into the editors' hands or their growing emphasis on the magazine as an historical repository forced poetry to take a back seat. The "Parnassiad", which had earlier been one of the most vital media for American verse in its day, eroded into a refuge for imitative, sterile verse.

The theoretical objections to fiction described in the previous chapter did not preclude its publication in the *Columbian*. In fact, Frank Luther Mott has called the magazine one of the most significant repositories of fiction in eighteenth-century America.[18] Like its counterparts, the *Columbian* side-stepped Scotch Realism's metaphysical objections to fiction by claiming that its stories were real.[19] Most of its fiction was titled "The History of . . ." or professed to be "Based on fact". Titles such as "The History of Kitty Wells: a True Story", "The Shipwreck; A Fragment Founded on Fact", "The Prisoner; A Sentimental Morsel Founded on a Fact still existing in the Gaol of Philadelphia", "Amelia; or the Faithless Briton: An Original Novel, Founded upon Recent Facts", "The History of Mr. Wilfort (A True Narrative)", "The Story of Altmont and Arabella: Founded on facts, which occurred in New Jersey during the late war" disguised supernatural and sentimental tales under the cloak of American reality. These tearful tales of seduction, sorrow, and premature death are obviously indebted to the school of sentimentality which followed Richardson, Mackenzie, and Sterne. The fact that several were acknowledged to be "Translated from the French" seems to support Ernest Baker's contention that French sentimental novelists Nicholas Etienne Framery, Madame de la Fayette, and the Abbe Prevost actively influenced the course of sentimental fiction in both England and America.[20]

American publication. The poem was apparently a popular bit of American antiquarianism, for it was also mentioned in Samuel Kettell, *Specimens of American Poetry* (Boston, 1829), I, xviii.

[18] *A History of American Magazines*, I, 96.

[19] This was the common practice of the time. See Martin, *The Instructed Vision*, 126 ff.

[20] *The History of the English Novel* (New York, 1957), V, 121-129 and 146.

But sentimentality was not the only mood of American fiction during the early national period. The *Columbian* printed a sizeable body of Oriental tales, allegories, and prose renderings of poetry. Interestingly enough, the pure Gothic is absent, although there are Gothic elements in sentimental novels. No stories anticipate the domestication of Gothic terror later achieved by Charles Brockden Brown.

Herbert R. Brown finds two strains of influence in eighteenth-century American sentimental fiction – that of Richardson and that of Sterne. To Richardson he ascribes the stock characters and situations of the novel of seduction: the seduced maiden, the attractive libertine, mercenary parents, and a system of poetic justice; to Sterne, the prevalence of tearful sensibility and emotional humanitarianism. The considerable body of sentimental fiction produced in America from 1785 to 1800 grew, he believes, from these two influences.[21]

Most of the short fiction in the *Columbian* belongs to one or the other of these divisions of sentimental fiction, although they frequently overlap. Interestingly enough, neither Sterne nor Richardson exerted much stylistic influence over the authors of these tales. Only one story, "Ela: or the Delusions of the Heart" in September 1788, was epistolary, perhaps because the magazine could not afford the luxury of the leisurely unfolding of plot necessitated by letter form.[22] Similarly, the playful style of *Tristram Shandy* appeared only in "The Virtuoso" (Supplement I, December 1787). But Richardson's stereotypes and Sterne's rhetoric of sensibility mark most of the fiction in the magazine.

The *Clarissa Harlowe* archetype dominates a number of stories. In most cases the parents' failure to give their daughters proper education rather than their mercenary motives betrays the girl's virtue, although in "The History of Leander and Matilda" (January 1790) Matilda's mother urges her to marry the rakish

---

[21] *The Sentimental Novel in America 1789-1860* (Durham, N. C., 1940), *passim.*

[22] Jeremy Belknap's *The Foresters* was converted to epistolary form when it appeared in book format in 1792, but when serialized in the *Columbian* during 1787 and 1788 it was a conventional narrative.

Lotherio because of his fortune. The father in "The History of Melidor and Clarinda; *or the Progress of Infidelity*" (November 1791) recommends the rake to his daughter because both Voltaire and Bolingbroke, whom he admires, were rakes in youth and because Melidor is a deist. Amelia, heroine of "Amelia; or the Faithless Briton" (October 1787 through Supplement I, December 1787) is seduced by a fake wedding ceremony.[23] But the coquettes who are the heroines of "The Flirt: A Moral Tale" (June 1791) and "Eugenia – Or the Coquette" (November 1792) lose their virtue because their mothers have planted in their heads false ideas of their prospects and worth. The authors suggest that, like the famous Elizabeth Whitman, these girls are seduced by their own pride.

Closest to the prototype of the Lovelacean villain is Doliscus, the wounded British officer whom Amelia nurses back to health in "Amelia; or the Faithless Briton". "Reared in the school of dissipation", Doliscus deserts the pregnant heroine on Long Island and, when she follows him to London, turns her friendless into the streets during an evening of drunken debauchery. After her insanity and death, he dies with Lovelacean relief on

[23]   Lillie B. Loche, *The Early American Novel* (New York, 1930), 61, points out that "Amelia" is the earliest truly American tale of the Revolution. A case could be made for its being the first American novel. Its publication in the *Columbian* in 1787 preceded by two years the appearance of William Hill Brown's *The Power of Sympathy*, which is generally considered the first American novel. So popular was "Amelia" that it was pirated by the *Massachusetts Magazine* in 1789 and by the *New York Magazine* in 1795. It was printed in book form in 1798 along with another short novel which first appeared in the *Columbian*, "Amelia; or Malevolence Defeated". The book was published in Boston by William Spotswood, who was proprietor of the *Columbian* when both tales appeared there during the late summer of 1787. The close connection of the two stories suggests that they may have had the same author. The book identifies "Amelia; or Malevolence Defeated" as the work of "A Lady of Massachusetts". If so, the stories are probably the work of Mrs. Sarah W. Morton's circle of novelists who made the *Massachusetts Magazine* the shrine of sentimental fiction in America. Among them were Susannah Rowson, William Hill Brown, James Butler (author of *Fortune's Foot-ball*), and Hannah Foster. See Loche, 15 and Brown, *The Sentimental Novel in America*, 8-11.

the sword of her brother. Another Lovelace figure, Melidor, breaks down Clarinda's Puritan chastity by the power of his manners and by teaching her deism.

One American Clarissa has the misfortune to marry her Lovelace. Although Matilda loves Leander, who is away fighting in the Revolutionary army, her mother orders her to marry the debauched Lotherio, who treats her brutally on their wedding night, regards her "as the slave of his appetites", and spends his time in taverns with other women. Although seduced only technically, Matilda suffers all the shame and anguish of the fallen maiden and fits the Clarissa prototype spiritually if not literally.

Other stories seem to exist only as excuses for rhetorical outpourings of sensibility. The author of "The History of Oliver; or, the Triumph" (August 1791) weeps lofty generalities over the humanitarianism of his hero Oliver Emerson: "Amidst the various instances of human depravity, to which we daily are witnesses, the truly civilized mind dwells with rapture on sentiments and actions, which evince the graces of humanity, and the dignity of virtue". In other tales the personal distresses of characters move the sensibilities of author and reader. The heroine of "Honoria: Or, the Mourner Comforted" (December 1792) stops in mid-narration to shed a tear over her dead lover Sylvanus. She resumes to tell of how his frequent overnight visits to her home and her illness after his death caused her to be slandered and her parents to die of shame. Only after her name was cleared did she consent to marry an old family friend and prove that "injured merit is often triumphant even in this world".

The most pathetic tale of sensibility in the magazine is "The History of Miranda and Cleander. *An American Tale*" (December 1790). "Ah! Britain!" the author begins, "behold, in this mournful tale, some of the sad effects of thy cruel tyranny, and let remorse set bourds to thy ravages in future! Ye nations, who sacrifice, at the shrine of accursed ambition, myriads of the human race, attend to my artless narrative, and learn to revere the sacred rights of Humanity!" The author continues to tell of a frontier beauty, a paragon of virtue and intelligence, whose lover joins the Revolutionary Army. The British stir a band of marauding Indians to massacre the settlement: "the women, their superior delicacy considered, expire in still greater agonies. Miranda dies, the victim of barbarity; and the tresses of beauty constitute a part of the triumph of a savage." Her lover Cleander leads the American troops in revenge, but is killed himself in the battle. "Expiring, he was heard to say, that 'The reward of virtue can be expected in heaven alone'." The narration is interspersed by, and seems merely an excuse for, the author's display of his sensibility and his rhetorical moralizing.

These tales of sensibility solicit the "tear of the reader" by describing the emotions of the characters in rhetorical detail. Miranda weeps when Cleander leaves for war, and he, upon learning of her being scalped, faints. The lovers in "The Story of Altmont and Arabella" (November 1790) react even more violently to wartime separation: "He rushes to war. – The tumult of passion swells in the bosom of Arabella. – She utters the involuntary scream – she faints .– ... His heart was divided between love and glory. Love exacted his sighs and anguish; but patriotism, in the breast of the hero, supersedes all other considerations." Seduced and deserted American Clarissas possessed equally keen sensibilities. Amelia, upon learning that Doliscus had deserted her, exclaimed " 'Gracious God!' ... and fell senseless to the ground." Later she falls into an Ophelia-like madness and, seated in bed surrounded by flowers, sings a melancholy song of seduction, desertion, and death.

Mackenzie's man of feeling is best illustrated by the hero of "The History of Leander and Matilda". Not only did he see his sweetheart marry a rake while he was away at war, he himself later wed a flirt who proved an adulterous wife and, subsequently, a whorish widow. After he and Matilda meet and tell one another of their unhappy marriages, he weeps bitterly and returns home to blow out his brains.

This accumulated image of sordid sexuality was softened by the moral sensibility of characters and authors. Clarinda, the girl seduced by the deistic rake, teaches her bastard child the precepts of true virtue and religion and tells her story to warn other girls from being drawn into (in the words of another heroine) "the vortex of vice". The "History of Oliver" teaches that "the virtues of the heart are not restricted to any climate or colour, and that the man who is industrious, grateful, and benevolent, must conciliate the permanent esteem of the worthy and enlightened part of mankind". At the conclusion of "The Story of Altamont and Arabella" the reader is exhorted to "rejoice in the triumph of honour, and the disgrace of treachery". "The Prisoner; a Sentimental Morsel founded on a Fact; still existing in the Gaol of Philadelphia", who has been jailed for debt, warns: "Think well, ye creditors! The abuse of power is base: though tolerated *here*, how will it be *hereafter*?" Such an obvious show of moral sensibility helped these tales subvert the accusation that fiction stimulated the base appetites and lowered the morals of its readers.

Although of little literary merit itself, the sentimental fiction in the *Columbian* confirmed the taste for sensibility in American readers. These tales are the American harvest of Richardson, Sterne, and Mackenzie, and in turn the seeds of the more skilfully executed novels of Susannah Rowson, Hannah Foster, Ann Bleecker, and a circle of other female novelists in the 1790's. Moreover, they began the love of sentimental sex which has dominated American popular culture from the gift book to the television screen.

Judging by the frequency of their appearance, Oriental tales appealed to the readers of the *Columbian* only slightly less than literary seduction. Theoretically, the Oriental tale was even better suited to the editors' theory of fiction. First, the locale of the story was so obviously removed from reality that the reader could not confuse its fictional possibilities with the actuality of American life; thus the Scotch metaphysical objection to fiction was largely obviated. Secondly, the Oriental tale was traditionally didactic.

Of the four types of Oriental tale,[24] only the moral and the philosophical appear in the *Columbian*. The imaginative, based on the *Arabian Nights*, was too romantic for post-revolutionary

[24]   Martha Pike Conant, *The Oriental Tale in England in the Eighteenth Century* (New York, 1908), originally classified the oriental tale into four types, which were accepted by Baker, *History of the English Novel*, V, Chapter 3.

American taste; and the satiric, best illustrated by Goldsmith's employment of the visitor from an alien land in the *Chinese Letters*, traditionally criticized the existing culture, which the standard of American nationalism would not allow. More congenial to the American taste for didacticism were the moral and philosophical tales, which came from the English periodical essay – particularly from Addison, Steele, and Johnson – and which taught the precepts of English neoclassicism.

The moral tales in the magazine reveal a Christian, and in one case an almost Puritan, attitude. "Eastern Generosity" (January 1790) plays upon the Golden Rule and teaches that virtue is rewarded. The Caliph's lieutenant of police rescues a Damascene prisoner who had earlier saved him in battle. Dr. Anthony Trumbull's "Visions of Aleph" (January 1789) combines a Puritan condemnation of sensuality and a lavishly sensual description reminiscent of Milton's prelapsarian Adam and Eve in Paradise. In the tale the Caliph Aleph tells his son of the lures of sexual pleasure and of the vision of heavenly beauty offered him by an angel. Aleph rejected Heaven for sex and received the curse of the Son of Heaven. Dying, Aleph gives his family a stern warning to reject earthly pleasures and look only to God; but he describes his vision of Heaven in lavish earthly sensuality:

The tops of the mountains were then edged with gold, and their soft shades stretched along the valley; the leaf of each spray hung with pearls of dew; the birds of every tree raised the voice of praise; the cooing turtle bill'd with its mate: life, love and joy were diffused; and every grove sung the song of delight. As we walked on the boarders of the mead, the flowers sprang to kiss thy feet, and the breeze came to catch thy fragrant breath. (p. 20)

The lavishness here is less Oriental than Miltonic; nevertheless, its sensuous imagery does temper the Puritan moral somberness of the rest of the tale. In another vein, "Temperance and Content" (December 1789) teaches that parents must educate their children to be proof against the temptations of wealth and sensuality.

The philosophical tales teach balance, harmony, and the wisdom of being content with what one has, in imitation of Johnson's *Rasselas*. In the "Complaint of Iman" (October 1787), Iman, discontented with a world in which evil seems to triumph over good, sees a vision of the balance Providence gives to all men. The rich and powerful are jealous of those richer and more powerful and are anxious because their hate is reciprocated; whereas the poor are happy with what little pleasures they find. The moral stated at the end is that "Providence has granted a proportionate share of misery and felicity to every mortal. . . ." "Royalty, an Eastern Tale" (April 1787) teaches the same lesson through a similar vision.

The longest of the Oriental tales in the *Columbian*, "Bathmendi" (January 1787), tells of four brothers who are told to seek Bathmendi. The three eldest set out in quest, but the youngest, who distrusts the seer who gave the advice, marries a neighbor's daughter and settles down to a life of farming. After lives of misery and wandering, the three elder brothers return home to find Bathmendi, the Persian word for happiness, a guest in their brother's home.

Interestingly enough, the philosophical and social principles of the American Revolution were never presented in the Oriental form. Apparently American authors could not shape it to contemporary problems. Equally devoid of contemporary allusion were the allegories appearing in the magazine, although several were by American authors. Most of these performances lack art and imagination; their characters are bloodless abstractions drawn only occasionally in human likeness. The "Birth of Hope: An Allegory" (August 1791) tells of the marital incompatibility of the slow and timid Fear and the resolved and precipitate Confidence. Jupiter grants them a divorce, but not before a daughter, Hope, who combines the best qualities of both, is born. The equally artificial "Prudence and Artifice" (June 1791) tries to show how Prudence rules Passion and teaches mankind industry, religion, and political improvement.

To the February, March, and April 1791 magazines, Elizabeth Graeme Fergusson contributed a highly disorganized and obscure "Allegory composed for the use and attention of young people; to impress upon their minds a nice regard to Wisdom and Truth", which she had composed some years earlier for the instruction of her niece and nephew Ann and John Young. In the story False-hood moves into the neighborhood with the happy couple Wisdom and Truth and dupes Wisdom into an adulterous relationship with her which brings about the couple's divorce and the birth of Cunning. Within this tangled weg of vague events Mrs. Fergusson recommends to the young kindness to animals, a proper regard for education, and the wisdom of morality. One of the more interesting features of the allegory is Mrs. Fergusson's use of scenes from the American Revolution to counter the misleading images of classical mythology. When Falsehood attempts to corrupt the children of the neighborhood by showing them pictures of "*Venus* rising from the sea" or "*Semele* waiting the descent of *Jove*", Wisdom offers "*Wolfe*, in his last moments, as drawn by the pencil of *West*" and "*Warren*, as touched by the hand of *Trumbull*" in what is perhaps the most ingenious use of the idea of the moral superiority of American life in the pages of the magazine.

Allegorical treatments of social issues normally appear in the form of dream visions, another type of fiction likely derived from the periodical essay. "A Dream" (January 1789) imagined that people were turned into fish and equated different social and political types with different species: "Swindlers, contractors, usurers, pettifoggers – and especially professional soldiers" became sharks, absolute rulers became vulnerable whales, beaux and belles became painted dolphin. The author satirized female fashions by describing a deformed fish with humps like a camel, which turned out "to be simply a cat-fish, with two unhappy protuberances, resembling those of a modern Venus, commonly called the gorge and the bishop". Among the other dreams treating social issues were "The Benefits of Charity" (August 1787), in which the author was transported to heaven and allowed to view the doomsday book, from which he learned that Philadelphia was to be destroyed by fire in May 1788 unless free schools were established by that time; and Benjamin Rush's "Paradise of Negro-Slaves" (January 1787), in which the narrator dreamed he was in a country inhabited only by Negroes who told him tales of the atrocities which sent them to their deaths. The piece ends with the appearance of Quaker humanitarian Anthony Benezet, whom the Negroes greet as their savior. These "dreams" recommended to their readers specific courses of social action presented in fictional form to increase their emotional appeal.

The most extensive allegory in American literature, Jeremy Belknap's *The Foresters,* was serialized in the *Columbian* from June 1787 through April 1788. Based on Dr. Arbuthnot's *The History of John Bull,* Belknap's allegory traces the history of the settlement of North America from its discovery through the establishment of the government of the United States after the Revolution. Although more noted for its historical accuracy than its literary quality, Belknap's work is an ingenious attempt at a sustained translation of all the salient features of American history into allegorical images.

Another type of prose fiction imitated Ossian. Several highly romantic set pieces pictured heroes about to leave for battle gushing their emotions in a heightened heroic style complete with Homeric simile and rhetorical sensibility. A variation of the Ossianic style appeared in a sketch in February 1787 in which a man in deep grief receives momentary consolation by wandering over the hills of his estate reading Ossian. The appearance of these fragments and the printing of portions of Lessing's "The Furies" in September 1792 indicates an embryonic romanticism in American thought as the nineteenth century approached.

Although, for the most part, the fiction printed in the *Columbian* was highly imitative of its English cousin, the obvious popularity of the tales of sensibility in spite of theological and metaphysical opposition, the appearance of occasional passages of lavish emotionalism in otherwise moralistic Oriental tales, and the interest in pre-romantic fiction indicate that American taste was changing and that public acceptance of fiction was eminent.

The pervasive influence of the Addisonian essay stretches through a century of American literature from Franklin's Silence Dogood to Irving's Jonathan Oldstyle, but nowhere is it more deeply evident than in the magazines of the early national period.[25]

[25]   Ernest C. Coleman, "The Influence of the Addisonian Essay in America before 1810" (University of Illinois Ph.D. dissertation, 1936) has traced

The *Columbian Magazine* printed five periodical essay series during its life. One, "The Economist", died after only one issue in July 1791 and another, the two-part "Improver" was clipped from a New Jersey schoolboy publication. But the other three are significant contributions to the genre in America.

"The Trifler" ran for 11 numbers sporadically between December 1786 and August 1788. It was apparently the work of a single unidentified author who signed the first number "Y. Germantown". The second "Trifler" did not appear until June 1787, but thereafter the series was a monthly feature of the magazine, missing only the October and December 1787 and the February 1788 numbers until it was discontinued in August 1788. Another, "The Retailer", ran for 16 months from February 1788 through March 1790. It seems to have been the work of at least four authors, only one of whom, Charles Crawford, can be identified with any degree of probability.[26] A third, the four numbers of Charles Brockden Brown's "Rhapsodist", signed *B, R, O,* and *W*, appeared in August, September, October, and November 1789.

The "Retailer" openly acknowledged his debt to Addison, Steele, Johnson, and Hawkesworth and occasionally cited the example of the *Spectator, Rambler,* and *Observer* to justify the subject matter of his essays.[27] The other essayists borrowed without his candor. All their essays are replete with the typical devices of the English periodical essay. They begin with a characterization of the persona and a sketch of the club he represents. The "Retailer" claims to be one who displays the wares of his club, which consists of a punster, a Sancho Panza

---

this influence in detail through early American newspapers and magazines and has demonstrated that the *Spectator* was the principal model for the profusion of periodical essays appearing in these publications. Guy Cardwell, "The Influence of Addison and Steele on Charleston Periodicals, 1788-1860", *Studies in Philology*, XXXV (1938), 456-470, describes a similar influence in Charleston, South Carolina, periodicals and concludes that the Addisonian essay was the greatest single literary influence in antebellum Charleston.

[26] "Retailer" No. XIII (November 1789) is signed "C. C.", Crawford's usual signature for pieces he submitted to the *Columbian*.

[27] See April 1788, 202-206 and December 1788, 695-698, for example.

who repeats proverbs, a connoisseur of dress, a ladies' man, and a politician. The "Trifler" defines himself as one "who collects facts and compiles materials, merely for his own solitary rumination, . . . and, having employed great part of a long life in various and unconnected literature, he is anxious to make atonement by endeavouring, tho' late, to leave to his country, some of those monitory legacies which his reading and experience will enable him to do" (December 1786, pp. 164-165). Although he does not represent a club, the "Trifler" frequents a local tavern and often reports the conversations of the characters there.

Whereas these personae are obviously derived from the *Spectator* and the *Tatler*, Brown's "Rhapsodist" represents a more purely romantic outlook.[28] He says of himself: "A rhapsodist is one who delivers the sentiments suggested by the moment in artless and unpremeditated language. His reasoning is always introduced to illustrate the circumstance, and the fact to confirm the reasoning. He pours forth the effusions of a sprightly fancy, and describes the devious wanderings of a quick but thoughtful mind . . ." (August 1789, p. 467). Brown's emphasis on imagination and on the free wandering of an inspired mind contrasts to the classical wit and controlled prose of the "Retailer" and the "Trifler". Moreover, the "Rhapsodist" is an enemy to human society and displays an affinity with physical nature which anticipates Wordsworth's description of the human mind as "naturally the mirror of the fairest and most interesting properties of nature" Says Brown of his "Rhapsodist":

He loves to converse with beings of his own creation, and every personage, every scene, is described with a pencil dipt in the colours of imagination. To his strong and vivid fancy, there is scarcely a piece of mere unanimated matter existing in the universe. His presence inspires, being, instinct, and reason into every object, real or imagined, and the air, water and the woods, are thronged with innumerable inhabitants. (September 1789, p. 537)

---

[28]   Harry R. Warfel, in his introduction to the Scholars' Facsimiles and Reprints edition of *The Rhapsodist and Other Uncollected Writings* (New York, 1943), p. vii, suggests that the mood of the essays is not pure romanticism, but rather reflects Brown's own withdrawal during the years in which he was studying law in the office of Alexander Wilcocks.

This statement of the powers of the imagination is stronger and more radical than Freneau's tenuous probings two decades earlier and adumbrates the spirit of Poe. So radically different was Brown's "Rhapsodist" from the accepted canon of taste in periodical essays that he drew a rebuke from the "Retailer", who said that "a *Rhapsodist* is a very extraordinary character, whom everybody suffers to do as he pleases, because nobody cares for him" (February 1790, p. 92). Brown did find the "affusions of a sprightly fancy" difficult to sustain in a monthly paper; the quality of the "Rhapsodist" declined sharply after two issues and the series ceased after four. But few contrasts in the early national period point so vividly to the transition occurring in American taste than do the attitudes and styles of the "Retailer" and the "Rhapsodist".

The longer periodical essays in the magazine found typical Addisonian devices indispensable. The whole of "Retailer" No. II was a fictitious letter from an Englishman who made fun of English travelers in America. The "Trifler" managed to postpone his recourse to letters until the third issue but found it so sucessful that the third and fourth numbers are composed entirely of letters. Both essayists also imitated the topical matter of the English periodical essays. An Oriental tale appeared in "Retailer" No. IV; "Retailer" No. XIII and "Trifler" No. V attacked the pretensions of literary societies; the foibles of fashion provided satire for "Retailer" Nos. XIV, XV, and XVI; and "Trifler" Nos. VI, VIII, and X classified social types. The "Trifler" was, for the most part, imitative, stilted, and dull; but the "Retailer" occasionally achieved distinction by the application of the traditions of the periodical essay to American life, and particularly by his use of native American humor.

Many essays which were not a part of a periodical series followed the *Spectator* model, especially those which satirized fashions and manners. Essays instructing the young in courtship, humorous letters describing the fashions of city or country people, and mock orations on the value of rum or of the potato relieved the seriousness of discussions of morals, government, or science. Benjamin Rush's "On the Different Species of Mania" (December

1786) treats human obsessions with horses, hunting, gambling, machines, dress, militarism, ecclesiasticism, and virtuosity as humorous diseases to be cured by the physician Reason. But more often, the single essays are serious and resemble rhetorical school exercises or the precise prose of scientific inquiry. The American essay was still under the firm control of the English example.

The popularity of three literary genres – biography, history, and geographical and topographical description – was stimulated by American nationalism. The successful termination of the Revolution created in America a curiosity about the past, present, and future of the new nation that could best be satisfied by these forms of writing. Also, these genres were philosophically more acceptable than fiction and poetry because they dealt with the actual rather than with the imaginary.

Biography was one of the first genres to flourish on American soil. Seventeenth-century Puritans memorialized God's Providences in New England by chronicling the lives of their saints. The achievement of independence gave the form a powerful impetus. According to Donald Stauffer one of the major trends in English biography in the eighteenth century was the choice of more democratic heroes.[29] The Revolution provided American biographers with such heroes and with eyewitness accounts and contemporary records of their deeds. The beginning of the new nation also aroused public interest in the first settlers of the continent.[30] Antiquarians like Jeremy Belknap found in the historical records of New England material easily exploited for magazine publication.

To the men who wrote for the *Columbian*, the purpose of biography, as of all literature, was to present an example of morality or heroism to instruct the reader. Belknap, in the preface to his "American Plutarch" series, quoted Lord Clarendon on the

[29]   *The Art of Biography in Eighteenth Century England* (Princeton, 1941), 456.
[30]   See Spencer, *The Quest for Nationality*, 14 ff for a discussion of this aspect of literary nationalism.

usefulness of a collection of the lives of great men as a guide for the present age and continued:

In deference to the judgment of such an attentive observer of mankind, and trusting that this country is capable of affording instances of such "heroic and virtuous men" as ought to be remembered and celebrated; we shall endeavour to present to the view of our readers, from time to time, some memoirs of the lives and characters of the founders of the American States, and of such other persons as have made a principal figure in them, compiled from the best materials within reach. (January 1788, p. 3)

Other writers followed Belknap's example. In the events of America's past, particularly in the acts of Revolutionary heroes, Americans found patterns of greatness which created a sense of national unity and pride. The didactic purpose of literature assumed a new dimension to the writer conscious of the national spirit, and virtue became, in the words of one biographer, "republican virtue".

Biographies appeared in the *Columbian* in three forms. First was the brief thumbnail sketch. At the close of the Revolution, a number of men, including Jeremy Belknap, believed that compiling a collection of American biographies comparable to the eighteenth-century English collections of the lives of religious leaders, authors, and public figures [31] would help crystallize national spirit. Their sketches concentrated on a single aspect of their subject's life and personality and in many instances described his Ruling Passion. In the case of Samuel Adams the passion was a love for his country; with Jefferson, his intellectual versatility; with Benezet his benevolence. The biographers attempted no comprehensive physical description or survey of the subject's life.

A second form of biography was the longer character sketch complete within a single issue of the magazine and varying in length from three to ten pages. These biographies dwelt upon the subject's central contribution to national life and imitated the style and organization of short biographies appearing in *Gentleman's Magazine*. Alexander Macwhorter's sketch of the life of

[31] Stauffer, *The Art of Biography*, 458.

William Livingston discussed the subject's efforts on behalf of civil and religious liberty, his sermons opposing the stamp act, his political writings during the first stages of the conflict with Britain, and his service in the Continental Congress and as Governor of New Jersey as concrete proof of his "republican virtue". The biographer's style combined concrete events and rhetorical praise.

The third form surveyed chronologically the major events in the subject's life. These biographies ranged in length from Carey's two-part "Sketch of the Life of the Late Nathaniel Greene" in September and October 1786 to Henry Stuber's "History of the Life and Character of Benjamin Franklin", which appeared in almost every monthly issue from May 1790 through June 1791. Nearer the average were Belknap's "American Plutarch" biographies, each of which appeared over three or four issues. Although characterization played a part in these serial biographies, it was incidental to the narrative. Only those events directly related to the subject's experience as an American were presented: for example, Belknap ignored Captain John Smith's Turkish adventures.

The sources of the biographical material varied. The "Portrait of General Washington" which appeared in January 1787 was "Translated from the French of Mr. Mandrillon, by a very young lady." David Humphreys got the material for his life of General Israel Putnam from personal remembrances, from Rev. Samuel Peters' *History of Connecticut,* from a series of anecdotes collected by Putnam's physician, Dr. Albigence Waldo, and from the military records he found at Mount Vernon during his residence there.[32] Belknap depended for his material upon the early histories of New England compiled by William Hubbard, Cotton Mather, and Thomas Prince; upon the writings of Captain John Smith and the English travel collection *Purchas His Pilgrims;* and upon such letters, state papers, books, and newspapers as he and his friends could turn up.[33] Many of the biographies came from the

[32] Leon Howard, *The Connecticut Wits* (Chicago, 1943), 243-244.
[33] On several occasions Belknap requested specific information from his friend Hazard. See "Belknap Papers", 5th Ser., II, 500 and III, 90.

author's personal acquaintance with his subject, as was the case of Benjamin Rush's life of Francis Hopkinson in May 1791.

The most interesting biographical source was Henry Stuber's use of the holograph manuscript of Franklin's *Memoirs* for his "History of the Life and Character of Benjamin Franklin".[34] The first two parts of Stuber's biography are a detailed paraphrase of the *Memoirs* text from its beginning to Franklin's first arrival in Philadelphia. For many pages Stuber simply changed Franklin's "I" to "he" and made minor alterations in the diction and punctuation to bring Franklin's style into closer correspondence with rhetorical principles. The following examples will illustrate the nature of Stuber's alterations:

Holograph MS (Farrand, pp. 18 and 20)	Stuber (May 1790, p. 271)
But my Father in the mean time, from a View of the Expence of a College Education which, having so large a Family, he could not well afford, and the mean Living many so educated were afterwards able to obtain, Reasons that he gave to his Friends in my Hearing, altered his first Intention, took me from the Grammar School, and sent me to a school for Writing & Arithmetic kept by a then famous Man, Mr. Geo. Brownell . . .	But his father, considering that with his large family he could ill afford the expenses of a collegiate education, and that persons so educated were often poorly provided for, removed him from the grammar school to a school for writing and arithmetic. This school was kept by a Mr. George Brownell, who was celebrated as being generally sucessful in teaching. . . .

[34] That Stuber's biography is based on the holograph manuscript rather than one of the fair copies made by Benny Bache is apparent from a textual comparison. In several cases Stuber keeps a reading which Bache altered. For example, Franklin's statement that his early ballads were "in the Grubstreet ballad stile", the William Temple Franklin text, which is taken from one of the fair copies, omits. Stuber includes the phrase in exact quotation from the holograph manuscript. For a detailed comparison of the various texts of Franklin's autobiography, see Max Farrand, ed., *Benjamin Franklin's Memoirs* (Berkeley, University of California Press, 1949).

Holograph MS (Farrand, p. 32)	Stuber (May 1790, p. 272)
I now took a Fancy to Poetry, and made some little Pieces. My Brother, thinking it might turn to account encourag'd me, & put me on composing two occasional Ballads. One was called the *Light House Tragedy*, & contain'd an Acc^t of the drowning of Capt. Worthilake with his Two Daughters; the other was a Sailor Song on the taking of *Teach* or Blackbeard the Pirate. They were wretched stuff, in the Grubstreet Ballad Stile . . .	Franklin now took a fancy to poetry, and wrote several little poems. His brother thought this talent might be rendered advantageous, and persuaded him to write two ballads, the subjects of which he proposed. One was called the *Light House Tragedy*. It was founded on a melancholy accident, which had recently taken place, the drowning of Captain Worthilake and his two daughters. The other was a sailor song on the capture of *Teach or Blackbeard,* the noted pirate. It would undoubtedly afford much satisfaction to see these first productions of so celebrated a man. They probably contained no presages of his future greatness. *Dr. Franklin used to say, that they were wretched stuff, in the style of Grubstreet ballads.* [Last italics mine.]

There is no need to multiply examples. These quotations typify Stuber's manipulation of Franklin's manuscript by altering colloquial diction to more Latinate, by omitting parenthetical and qualifying phrases, by rearranging syntax to conform to the handbook grammar of the time, and by including direct quotations from the holograph manuscript under the guise of things Franklin "used to say", leaving the impression that Stuber himself heard them said.

After the first two serialized parts of his biography, Stuber followed the holograph manuscript less closely. It had become apparent that to cover Franklin's life in such detail would take far more space and time than Stuber or the magazine wished to allow. At the beginning of his biography, Stuber had apologized for the detail in which he was to discuss Franklin's boyhood, saying, "If, contrary to usual custom, we do not slightly pass over the early part of his life, let it be remembered that this is the period at which the mind received from education those impressions, and that character, which have the greatest influence upon later life" (May 1790, p. 269). Of course, Stuber's real reason was that the early years constituted the fullest and most animated part of his source. But when the details of Franklin's youth became too extensive, Stuber began summarizing the manuscript, still using it for his outline and dipping into its text on occasions to fill in details. Many events and details he omitted as unimportant. For the period of Franklin's life not covered in the manuscript, Stuber referred to the outline Franklin made when he began to write his memoirs. Not only did Stuber follow the order of events given in the outline, he misread a Franklin revision and perpetrated a mistake in facts. At one point in the outline Franklin had written: "Doctorate from Edinburg Doctorate from Oxford", but had later interlined the more specific "St. Andrews" after the word "Edinburg". Stuber mistakenly understood that Franklin had received three honorary degrees and wrote: "The University of St. Andrews, in Scotland, conferred upon him the degree of Doctor of Laws. Its example was followed by the Universities of Edinburgh and of Oxford." [35]

Stuber's biography is important not only because of its source but because Benjamin Vaughan in his 1793 *Works* of Franklin reprinted Stuber's material as a continuation of Franklin's *Memoirs*. Subsequent editors continued to print the last half of Stuber's biography under the name of Franklin's *Memoirs* until Jared Sparks corrected the error in his 1847 edition.[36]

[35] Farrand, p. 421 and *Columbian* (February 1791), 69. Franklin received only two honorary degrees from British institutions, one from St. Andrews in Edinburgh and one from Oxford. See Carl Van Doren, *Benjamin Franklin* (New York, 1938), 281-282 and 300.

[36] Paul Leicester Ford, *A Franklin Bibliography*, p. 181 contends, incorrectly, that Stuber wrote the biography especially for Benjamin Vaughan's edition. But Vaughan obviously pirated Stuber's work from a copy of the *Columbian* and did not know Stuber personally. Prefacing Stuber's continuation, Vaughan said: "We have thought proper, in order as much as possible to relieve his regret [that Franklin had not continued his memoirs], to subjoin the following continuation by one of the Doctor's intimate

The spirit of nationalism which followed the Revolution also generated a fascination with American history. Not only did American writers feel it necessary to defend their country against the charges of Buffon, the Abbe Raynal, and other Europeans that the American land was barren and unhealthy and the American people inferior to Europeans intellectually, physically, and socially, they, like their Puritan forefathers, believed it their duty to preserve for posterity an accurate record of the beginning of the nation which they believed would be the salvation of western man.

Moreover, the metaphysics of Scotch common sense realism supported their interest in history. The Scotch philosophers considered the writing of history the most useful of the arts because it depicts actual events in the lives of real people. Because the reader recognizes the heroes of history as real, he can experience an instructive impression of their virtue and heroism. This experience transcends the reading of fiction, which merely diverts the attention and amuses the mind.

The author of "On the Study of History" in the October 1792 *Columbian* contrasted history and fiction as follows: "The study of history requires some thought and attention, whereas the perusal of novels and romances claims not the least of either; the end of one is to improve the understanding, and correct the various passions of the human soul; that of the other, only to amuse" (p. 227). Following his philosophy, the "Impartial Review" acclaimed David Ramsay's *History of the Revolution of South-Carolina* and Jeremy Belknap's *History of New Hampshire*. The reviewer of Ramsay's book praised the author for accurately recording for posterity "the visible interference of Providence in favour of the cause of freedom" during the Revolution and regretted that similar records had not been written for all the states (September 1786, p. 23). Belknap's reviewer was heartened that the contemporaneous origin of American civilization saved American history from being obscured by poets and romancers,

---

friends. It was extracted from an American periodical publication, and was written by the late Dr. Stuber of Philadelphia." *Works of the Late Dr. Benjamin Franklin* (London, 1793), I, 190-191.

for the records of the founding of the nation were printed and available to the historian and would always be preserved to guide its citizens' conduct (February 1792, p. 111).

The publication of history in the *Columbian* took four forms. First, a large number of selections from early histories of New England dealing with the customs of the region during colonial times satisfied the readers' curiosity about American antiquities. Ancient laws and punishments seemed to attract the greatest interest, particularly laws concerning marriage, divorce, adultery, and personal property. Most of these articles were simply lists of unusual laws taken from the old histories and public records. For example, one article entitled "Curious Extracts from Ancient American Records" (November 1791) listed old laws from seven states, including such diverse items as a New York law to hang all Popish priests, a Massachusetts law fining any man who courts a woman without her parents' consent, a New Jersey law prescribing ten lashes on the bare backs of a man and woman who run off together, and a Maryland law forbidding the killing of an unmarked hog. Other articles included narrations of the founding of New England colleges (December 1788 and December 1792), an incident concerning the discovery of America (November 1791), and the experiences of three judges of King Charles I who spent their lives in hiding in New England (September 1788).[37]

Secondly, the interest of French anthropologists in the American Indian fostered the publication of several articles on the Red Man's history. Some, like "An Indian Tradition concerning the Origin of the Five Nations" from *Henry's Captivity* (October 1788), record oral legends. Others, like the extracts from Du Pratz's *History of Louisiana* (May 1788), linked the Indians to the Ten Lost Tribes of Israel.[38] One narrates the humorous attempt of an Indian woman and her white husband to get title to

[37] This incident became the source of Nathaniel Hawthorne's short story "The Gray Champion".

[38] Linking the American Indian and the Israelites was one method used by American nationalists to give the American continent a fabled antiquity usable as poetical association. See Lewis Hanke, *The First Social Experiments in America* (Cambridge, Mass., 1935), Appendix A for a detailed bibliography on the theory.

the entire territory of Georgia on the grounds that she was the rightful empress of the Creek nation (May 1788).

Materials about the history of the American Revolution appeared in two forms: primary historical documents and written histories. The printing of Washington's letters relative to the treatment of Captain Asgill, the publication of orations by Otis Warren and John Quincy Adams, and the first publication of letters written by John Adams on the eve of the signing of the Declaration of Independence make the *Columbian* a repository of primary historical documents. Even more significant are the state papers and official documents which became a regular feature of the magazine in its last months.

The most extensive written history was a serialized "History of the American Revolution" which ran from March 1789 through November 1792. Although forced to end with the Battle of King's Mountain because of the death of the magazine, it is the most detailed history of the war published in America within the first seven years after the close of the Revolution.

The source of the work and the policy of the author respecting his source are stated in its preface:

The following performance is not offered as entirely original. That admired publication, ascribed to Mr. Burke, which appeared in the Annual Register during the late war, affords, in the early periods of it especially, a variety of matter, which the writer of this Summary will make use of with little or no variation – convinced that where the matter accords with his own ideas, the superior elegance of its composition will justify the freedom he takes. He will often have occasion, however, to consult other authors; and to these resources he will add such other observations of his own as the opportunities of military life, in the war which he treats, have entitled him to make. *Truth* alone is his object, unbiased by any other view. (March 1789, p. 145)

Even when it copied Burke, the *Columbian* made minor changes in wording. These were apparently motivated by a desire to make the piece more congenial to an American viewpoint. For example, where Burke said that the rebellion "put an end to all established government" in the provinces, the *Columbian* stated that it "put an end to British rule". Where Burke said that Franklin was "disgraced and removed" from his post in England, the *Columbian* changed "disgraced" to "insulted".[39] In other places the *Columbian* departed from Burke entirely to narrate American triumphs in more detail. For an account of the war in the South, the magazine depended upon David Ramsay's *History of the Revolution in South-Carolina*, and sought details of other theaters of war in whatever documents it could find.

Almost all the historical writings in the magazine were obtained from other printed sources, which were reassembled by the editors. America had no tradition of interpretative historiography, and none could develop until a generation later when men like Francis Parkman and George Bancroft, trained in German graduate schools, brought the forces of scholarship and intellectual sophistication to bear on American history. But the *Columbian* did make the facts of America's past and present available to a national audience and to the historians who were to come after it.

The early national period also saw a birth of interest in the American landscape. Rhode Islanders, Pennsylvanians, and South Carolinians, suddenly united as a single nation, became curious about the environment and habits of their fellow countrymen, and the entire nation began to look westward toward the virgin lands between the Alleghenys and the Mississippi. By printing articles by such men as official national geographer Thomas Hutchins, Jedidiah Morse, and Gilbert Imlay, the *Columbian* fed the American appetite for knowledge of remote parts of the continent.

Topographical description appeared in both formal and informal essays. The formal essays assumed a scientific tone. The stylistic precision demanded by the Royal Society's proclamations on language encouraged exact descriptions of size and location. Writers like David Rittenhouse, who described the Ohiopyle

---

[39]   These passages are found in Edmund Burke, *An Impartial History of the War in America* (London, 1780), pp. 144 and 206 (the book collects the serial parts of Burke's history from the *Annual Register*), and the *Columbian* (July 1789), 336 and (February 1790), 115.

Falls in February 1787, avoided personal emotion and impression and dwelled on the mathematical description of nature:

The falls are, by estimation, about 20 feet in perpendicular height, and the river is perhaps 80 yards wide. For a considerable distance below the falls, the water is very rapid; and boils and foams vehemently, occasioning a continual mist to rise from it, even at noon-day, and in fair weather. The river at this place runs towards the S. W. but presently winds around to the N. W. and continuing this general course for 30 or 40 miles, it loses its name by uniting with the Monongahela, which contains, perhaps, twice as much water. (p. 284)

A similarly objective tone is found in the "Description of the Chalybeate Springs, near Saratoga" by G. Turner in March 1787. Turner describes the dimensions of the spring and speculates about the geological history of a large cone of rock which surrounds it. These and similar essays were accompanied by diagrams and copperplate engravings to facilitate the reader's understanding of the exact size and shape of the phenomenon being described.

Informal essays presented a subjective, personal description influenced by the rhetoric of the sublime and by Rousseauistic primitivism. Essays like Abraham Steiner's "Cursory Remarks made during a Short Journey from Hope, in Sussex-County, New-Jersey, to the Log-Gael, about seven miles distant from Hope" (July 1788) and the anonymous "Description of Bald Eagle Valley" (September 1788) emphasize the effect on the author's sensibility of the size, power, and grandeur of the scenes he views. In the most extreme instances, the images of nature are dissolved in the heat of the author's sensibility, leaving his rhetoric unsupported by concrete facts.

Occasionally, excerpts from works like Jefferson's *Notes on Virginia* and Bartram's *Travels* combined the observation of concrete nature and subjective meaning, but for the most part the topographical and geographical writing in the *Columbian* fell into one extreme or the other. As with the other literary genres in the magazine, descriptive writing failed to reconcile the conventional European forms and ideas which were its models with the essentially revolutionary sense of American nationalism which was demanded of it. Even so, geography, biography, and history were more congenial to American subject matter than the more belletristic pieces which appeared in the magazine. The periodical essay, the novel or short tale of manners, odes, elegies and *vers de société* with their suggestion of an established social order and a continuous tradition of manners and morals proved an awkward vehicle for national ideals of a republican society – unlimited growth and progress, maximum individual liberty, and freedom from the limitations of social tradition or past order. American nationalism demanded independence; but American authors had not yet learned how to achieve independence within tradition. Slavish imitation and an awkward dissociation of idea from form prevailed during the entire early national period and vitiated the literary quality of the *Columbian Magazine*.

IV

THE AMERICAN MUSE

Most of the belletristic material in the *Columbian Magazine* has no identifiable reference to American life. Images, characters, and settings either are generalized beyond individuality or are European. The conventions of the borrowed English genres hampered American writers seeking to portray their own country. Sophisticated American society so completely imitated London that American social satire seemed merely a branch of coffeehouse wit, and the magazine's editorial policy of avoiding the controversial, the personal, and the local at a time when local and personal controversy was one of the defining features of American life closed its pages to the most typically national subject matter of its time. Much of the literature in the magazine, in fact, can be called "American" only because it was written by Americans and published in an American periodical.

But many writers did attempt to support the *Columbian's* role as the organ of cultural nationalism by using American life as the subject matter of literature. Their achievement lacks intrinsic aesthetic merit; but it is important because they discovered America as a literary subject. Many of the themes, images, and characters through which nineteenth-century writers, among them Washington Irving, James Fenimore Cooper, and William Cullen Bryant, achieved the goal of a national literature made an early stumbling appearance in the pages of the *Columbian*.

The literary response to American nationalism was to seek themes and images which were uniquely American. In theory, at least, anything English was to be avoided. In practice, the result was often mixed. The most clearly unique feature of the new nation was its socio-political ideology, and polemic works such as the *Federalist* papers were its purest expression.[1] But more frequently authors superimposed the American ideology on stereotyped images copied from English models: for example, the clearly British heroine of the tale of sensibility who speaks passionately of American independence. In the language of T. S. Eliot, American writers failed to find an objective correlative suitable to express their social and political thoughts and feelings.

On the other hand, many writers found indigenous American images. The virgin land which seemingly stretched endlessly westward, the aboriginal inhabitant who roamed that land, the history of the white man's experience on the continent, the developing American character, and the promise of future national expansion gave writers themes and images to which English authors could lay no valid claim. These images were often revered for their Americanism rather than for their function and meaning within the structure of a literary work; but they were the beginning of American literature, and an understanding of their early use illuminates their later development in the hands of more skilled artists.

1. THE LAND

From the time of his first acquaintance with the New World, western man has viewed the American landscape through the lens of his own intellectual preconceptions. Images in classical literature of a western promised land – the Elysian Fields, the Hesperides, the Islands of the Blest, Lyonesse – and the desire of Christian theology in the late middle ages to find a new Eden to replace the crumbling order of the medieval world forced the earliest descriptions of the American land into the pattern of the pastoral idyll. At the same time, the reality of a wild and danger-

---

[1] Spencer, *Quest for Nationality*, 45. The relationship between political writing and belles lettres in the early national period has never been adequately studied.

ous nature in the New World gave the myth of the American garden a dark and sinister color.[2]

American nationalism and the intellectual currents of the eighteenth century shaped this polar view of American nature to their own characteristically optimistic temperament. Primitivism welcomed the pastoral New Eden; and the aesthetic idea of the sublime neutralized the dark face of the land. Man's fear of the vast, uncharted expanse of America's forests and the uncontrolled power of its rivers and waterfalls became sublimated into a cathartic experience. Rather than fearing American nature as a threat to his being, man found that it excited his sensibility; and the heightened emotional experience it produced purified him spiritually and morally.

The eighteenth century produced two amplifications on the aesthetics of the sublime which were particularly useful to the American artist. First, Edmund Burke identified the sublime with "whatever is fitted in any sort to excite the ideas of pain and danger, that is to say, whatever is in any sort terrible. ..." and said that subjects which are vast, massive, dark, and rugged and those which deviate from regularity and order produce the emotion of sublimity. Secondly, Hugh Blair insisted that the true source of the sublime is the object being described and that sublime language is simply the realistic description of a sublime object.[3] Whereas Longinus had emphasized sublime thought, emotion, and figurative language, Burke and Blair focused the author's attention on natural objects which possessed dimensions and features fearsome enough to excite pain and fear.

American mountains, rivers, waterfalls, and caverns offered a source of the sublime unparalleled in the experience of most English writers. Thomas Jefferson, describing the mountains and

---

[2]   Jones, *O Strange New World*, Chapters I, II, and III contains the most authoritative and detailed treatment of this dualism in American culture which many other scholars, including W. R. B. Lewis, have seen as central to our cultural history.

[3]   Edmund Burke, *A Philosophical Inquiry into the Origin of our Ideas of the Sublime and Beautiful*, quoted from Samuel Hynes, ed., *English Literary Criticism: Restoration and 18th Century* (New York, Appleton-Century-Crofts, 1963), 257. See also Blair, *Lectures*, I, 43.

rivers of Virginia, stated that the sublimity of the American scene was worth voyaging across the Atlantic to see (August 1787). The reviewer of David Humphreys' poem "On the Happiness of America" enumerated the sublime objects of the American landscape and suggested that viewing them could contribute to the delight and virtue of the American people:

The face of nature, throughout the United States, exhibits the *sublime and beautiful*, in the most exalted degree. In almost every part of this country, we are surrounded with objects calculated to inspire the most elevated conceptions of the imagination. Our mountains, vallies, plains, and rivers, are formed upon a great scale; the extent of the country itself is great; and the whole is rendered magnificently beautiful, by the creating hand of the Almighty Architect. (October 1786, pp. 67-68)

American writers utilized images of size, depth, and unharnessed power and the emotions surprise, terror, and awe to describe the American land. A good example of sublime description, unhampered by sentimental rhetoric, occurred in the "Description of Bald Eagle Valley". The author describes a cave in the region:

This opening in the hill continues about four hundred yards, when the cave widens, after you have got round a sudden turn, which prevents its being discovered till you are within it, to a spacious room, at the bottom of which is a vortex, the water that falls into it whirling round with amazing force; sticks, or even pieces of timber, are immediately absorbed, and carried out of sight, the water boiling up with excessive violence. (September 1788, p. 491)

The towering pine became a sublime image in "Verses Inscribed to Monmouth County" (August 1791), and the size and wildness of American nature provided images for "The Farmer" (October 1787). "Verses upon Gray's Ferry" not only used comparable imagery but created a myth to explain the sublimity of the American scene. On Parnassus the Muses complained to Jove of America's lack of poetic ability. In order to give American poets something to sing about, Jove created Gray's Ferry:

> Secure from summer's heat, and winter's storms;
> The rocks and woods adorn its bending sides,

> And Schuylkill here in gentle murmur glides:
> Above the rest two rocks of equal size,
> With their aspiring fronts assail the skies;
> The one ascended, yields the glorious sight,
> Where Delaware and Schuylkill's streams unite. . . .
> (August 1787, p. 607)

Converging rocks and rivers provided writers and landscape painters with sublime images for two generations. They form the background of Charles Brockden Brown's gothic novels and of James Fenimore Cooper's Leatherstocking Tales as well as a favorite subject for Hudson River School landscapes such as William Durant's "Kindred Spirits", which uses craggy rocks, a deep waterfall, and hazy, distant mountains to achieve the effect on canvas.[4]

In addition to using American images, several writers were inspired by the land to bursts of rhetoric which attempted to express the emotions stimulated by the landscape. The New Jersey countryside moved Abraham Steiner to a vision of the American Dream in which he proposed that such land would inevitably induce patriotism, morality, and reverence in its inhabitants:

Ah! thought I! Is there an hypochondriac, whose soul and body are afflicted with imaginary evils? . . . Is there a discontented mortal who can arraign the providence of his Creator, and the gratitude of his country? let him take such a walk, and see how bountifully God hath blessed the works of the labourer, and while he reviews the fertility of his country, let him examine his heart and sigh! (September 1788, pp. 502-503)

Steiner's faith in the restorative powers of nature anticipates the same theme in Bryant, whose belief was also based on the sublimity of the American land.

---

[4] Three recent articles relate Cooper personally and artistically with the Hudson River School: James F. Beard, "Cooper and His Artistic Contemporaries", *New York History*, XXXV (1954), 480-495; Howard Mumford Jones, "Prose and Pictures: James Fenimore Cooper", *Tulane Studies in English*, III (1952), 133-154; Donald A. Ringe, "James Fenimore Cooper and Thomas Cole: An Analogous Technique", *American Literature*, XXX (1958), 26-36. The same parallels apply to Brown and other writers whose descriptions are cast in the rhetoric of the sublime.

But sublimity alone was not enough. Many writers felt that the American landscape lacked the historical and emotional associations necessary to give their descriptions added significance, an attitude greatly strengthened by the influence of associational psychology and Scotch common sense realism in the early national period. Several complaints in the *Columbian* anticipated by forty years Cooper's statement that America lacked "the rich artificial auxiliaries of poetry" and Irving's observation, "no, never need an American look beyond his own country for the sublime and beautiful of natural scenery. But Europe held forth the charms of storied and poetical association." [5] In the June 1789 *Columbian* the author of "A Description of the Green Woods of Connecticut" admitted that "there is something wildly grand and characteristic in the rude scene we have described", but he complained that it was not in itself enough for the artist. The scene lacked the associations of "the castle, the abbey, or the villa, to draw [it] into consequence" (p. 366). The complaint stubbornly survived in American literature through Henry James's *Hawthorne* in 1876.[6]

Several of the *Columbian* authors circumvented the lack of association by comparing the American landscape to poetic Euro-

[5] *Notions of the Americans*, quoted from *James Fenimore Cooper: Representative Selections*, 16; Washington Irving, "The Author's Account of Himself", *The Sketch Book*, quoted from *Washington Irving: Selected Prose*, ed. Stanley T. Williams (New York, Holt, Rinehart and Winston, 1950), 82.

[6] After discussing the scarcity of material for a writer of Hawthorne's generation, James wrote: "This moral is that the flower of art blooms only where the soil is deep, that it takes a great deal of history to produce a little literature, that it needs a complex social machinery to set a writer in motion. American civilization has hitherto had other things to do than to produce flowers, and before giving birth to writers it has wisely occupied itself with providing something for them to write about." Henry James, Jr., *Hawthorne* (New York, 1879), 3. Hawthorne himself had voiced a similar complaint in the "Preface" to *The Marble Fawn* in 1860: "No author, without a trial, can conceive of the difficulty of writing a romance about a country where there is no shadow, no antiquity, no mystery, no picturesque and gloomy wrong, nor anything but a commonplace prosperity, in broad and simple daylight, as is happily the case with my dear native land." *The Complete Novels and Selected Tales of Nathaniel Hawthorne*, ed. Norman Holmes Pearson (New York, The Modern Library, 1937), 590.

pean scenes. The Reverend Peter Miller compared the limestone
caves of Swatara to a Gothic cathedral, thus achieving religious
associations to supplement the sublimity created by the vastness
of the caves (July 1787, p. 526). Gilbert Imlay pointed out that,
rather than being a virgin land, the Mississippi Valley had once
been as well cultivated and as thoroughly inhabited as the banks
of the Danube or the Rhine (March 1792, p. 180). The author of
"The former, present, and future prospects of America" claimed
with pride: "may we not see our rivers as superior to the babbling
brooks of the old continent in fame as in size, when neither the
Roman Tiber, nor the British Thames, shall surpass the gentle
Schuylkill, nor the more majestic Delaware?" (October 1786, p.
85). By this trick of juxtaposition, authors appropriated the
poetic associations of European objects rich in cultural history to
add texture to the American scene. Bryant was using the same
trick in 1832 when he wrote that on the American prairies

> . . . a disciplined and populous race
> Heaped, with long toil, the earth, while yet the Greek
> Was hewing the Pentelicus to forms
> Of symmetry, and rearing on its rock
> The glittering Parthenon.[7]

The second aspect of the medieval view of the New World, the
myth of the garden, became entangled with the eighteenth-
century doctrine of progress. Two conflicting views of nature's
role in the development of American life emerged from the
constitutional debate which raged in Philadelphia during the life
of the *Columbian*. Federalists saw nature as the raw material for
manufactures and cities; Jeffersonians viewed the fertile landscape
as a potential democratic agrarian paradise.

Jefferson believed that the future of America lay in what Leo
Marx has called the middle pastoral [8] – that is, nature tamed to

---

[7] "The Prairies", ll. 46-50.
[8] Leo Marx, *The Machine in the Garden* proposes the thesis that the central conflict in American culture is between the ideal of the pastoral and
the industrial development that threatens to doom it. "Hence", he says,
"the pastoral ideal is an embodiment of what Lovejoy calls 'semi-primi-
tivism'; it is located in a middle ground somewhere 'between,' yet in a

civilized uses but retaining its pastoral identity. To the writers of the early national period, the American land seemed so fecund that it could potentially support unlimited numbers of independent farmers who could pursue happiness and human dignity free from the degrading influences of urbanization.

The western territories gave Americans unlimited resources for development. Not even the most confined imagination could conceive of the frontier closed or its resources depleted. Captain Isaac Stuart praised Louisiana for:

The luxuriance of the soil, the richness of the herbage, the majesty of the forests, the richness of the meadows, which are in many places of amazing extent, and covered with rich grass and clover, that is in height, at least three feet. The woods are full of deer, elk, and buffaloe; and in the fall, grapes and apples are everywhere to be found. . . . (March 1787, p. 320)

David Ramsay assured Americans that the uncultivated lands to the west were limitless:

Such are the resources of your country, and so trifling are your debts, compared with your resources, that proper systems, wisely planned and faithfully executed, will soon fill your extensive territory with inhabitants, and give you the command of such ample capitals, as will enable you to run the career of national greatness, with advantages equal to the oldest kingdoms of Europe. (December 1791, pp. 375-76)

Dr. William Linn predicted the spread of agrarian civilization over the entire American continent and estimated that the western territory contained 200 million acres of land "inferior, in fertility, salubrity, and convenience, to no country upon earth" (September 1791, p. 189). Gilbert Imlay expressed the opinion that the sublimity of the Mississippi Valley was equalled only by the extent of the empire it was capable of supporting (November 1792, p. 308).

The western territory was not the only section of the country

---

transcendent relation to, the opposing forces of civilization and nature." (p. 23).

with great potential. William Bartram enthusiastically described the Alachua savanna of Georgia,

> ... whose exuberant green meadows, with the fertile hills which immediately encircle it, would, if peopled and cultivated after the manner of the civilized countries of Europe, without crouding or incommoding families, at a moderate estimation, accommodate in the happiest manner, above one hundred thousand human inhabitants, besides millions of domestic animals. (March 1792, p. 263)

Richard Champion in a book intended to lure emigrants to America, portions of which the *Columbian* printed in 1787 and 1788, described the Carolinas and Virginia as the paradise of the New World, whose "soil fertile, full of rich and pleasant vallies, finely wooded, and watered by continual springs" was capable of supporting cattle, grain, fruit, game, poultry, wine and oils superior to those produced in any part of Europe or Asia (October 1787, p. 686). Champion's imagery, like Stuart's, echoed the descriptions of the luxuriant Carolina landscape which Philip Amadas and Arthur Barlowe wrote in 1584 to bring the myth of the western garden to Elizabethan readers.

Such boundless natural resources made the ideal of the middle pastoral seem within easy reach and encouraged the dream of American perfectibility. Gilbert Imlay, after describing the vast commercial potential of the Mississippi Valley, remarked of its future settlers: "Thus, in the centre of the earth, governing by the laws of reason and humanity, we seem calculated to become at once the emporium and protectors of the world" (November 1792, pp. 310-311). Such pastoral idealism became an important part of the American Dream.

The city, too, was judged more on aesthetic than practical grounds, but the judgments were contradictory. On the one hand the city was a sublime object rivaling the most magnificent capitals of Europe. An anonymous author praised the Philadelphia State House (Independence Hall) for its superb architecture and for its association with American independence, which would make it "more interesting in the history of the world than any of the celebrated fabrics of Greece or Rome" (July 1787, p. 513). The new legislative structure in New York, in the eyes of another writer, equalled any building in Europe "for beauty of shades and polish" of the American marble used in decorating it (August 1789, p. 474). Alexander Ellicot said that the proposed city of Washington was built on "a tract of territory, exceeded, in point of convenience, salubrity, and beauty, by none in America". He also remarked that the plan of the city contained "important improvements upon that of the best planned cities in the world, combining, in a remarkable degree, convenience, regularity, elegance of prospect, and a free circulation of air"; and he predicted that the city "may be expected to grow up with a degree of rapidity hitherto unparalleled in the annals of cities" (March 1792, pp. 155-156).

Writers with Jeffersonian leanings, however, saw the city as the antithesis of the happy agrarian republic. The author of "The Farmer" called the city a den of vice, crowded conditions, and disease and preferred the open air of the country. He warned the urbanite:

> Yes, go, ye fools! to crowded towns repair,
> Immers'd in vice, go breathe polluted air;
> While pleas'd I wander o'er the bloomy vale,
> Where health rides laughing on the western gale. . . .
> (October 1787, p. 729)

A similar note was sounded by Charles Brockden Brown's "Rhapsodist", who found his removal from the banks of the Ohio to the grottoes of Philadelphia had distorted his brain and corrupted his imagination. Upon entering the crowded city, he said, "I experienced a temporary paroxism of phrenzy, my fancy was altogether ungovernable, and I frequently mistook the scene which was passing for the lively representation of a dream" (October 1789, p. 600). He longed to leave the "black despair" of the city and to return to the wilderness where his imagination could be governed by reason and not by the artificial garb of fashion.

Not only was the city unhealthy and vice ridden, it encouraged the worst abuses of democratic government. The author of "A Tour of the Eastern States" (September 1789) remarked that in the city of Newport, Rhode Island, the "beneficial regulation" of manners and morals was defeated by the democratic vote of a majority of the poorer element and "all the attempts of the virtuous minority for the public good, have been uniformly frustrated" (p. 534). Both Jeffersonians and Federalists tended to see the evils of the other faction in the face of the American city.

The American pastoral garden was largely a Jeffersonian vision. Federalist writers insisted that America must utilize nature as a resource for industrial and commercial expansion. This attitude is best represented in the *Columbian* by the large corpus of essays on the "useful arts" which comprise almost a quarter of the total contents of the magazine. Economic proposals, descriptions of new inventions, suggestions for utilizing natural resources more efficiently, and reports from the various Societies for the Promotion of the Useful Arts which sprang up in the aftermath of the Revolution dominated almost every issue of the magazine.

The two attitudes toward nature – as a spiritual resource and as a commercial resource – not only focused the conflict over the American identity from 1775 to 1825 but pointed toward a more significant later split in American culture. The practical, active American has seldom seen the aesthetic and spiritual side of nature, and the artist and intellectual has been appalled by the wanton destructiveness of those who view nature for its dollar value alone. The literary outcroppings of the conflict appeared in Mark Twain's nostalgia in *Life on the Mississippi* and in works like Frank Norris's *The Octopus* and *The Pit* in which the economic exploitation of nature became the central theme. But the pressures which produced the conflict were building during the years immediately following the Revolution, and the appearance of both attitudes toward nature in the *Columbian* helps explain the extent of the tradition behind their subsequent recurrence in literature and politics.

2. THE INDIAN

The ambivalent American attitude toward the Indian, like that toward the land, originated in Renaissance Europe. Theorists, who knew the Indian from a safe distance across the Atlantic, viewed him as an innocent, intelligent, admirable being. These early writers drew on Christian, classical, and pastoral imagery – the red man was Adam before the fall, the Latins before the arrival of Aeneas, shepherds in Arcadia, or residents of the Golden Age. On the other hand, to the Renaissance explorers, particularly the Spanish conquistadores, the Indian was a brutal, cannibalistic beast who must be eliminated before the land could be plundered of its wealth.[9]

As it entered literature, this paradox became even more emphatic. Montaigne's essay "Of Cannibals" crystallized the myth of the Noble Savage which proliferated in the eighteenth century into a major literary theme. From the appearance of the Indian in John Dennis's 1704 play *Liberty Asserted* and with increasing frequency throughout the century, writers in England and on the continent glorified the red man for exemplifying the natural nobility, courage, morality, and sympathy with nature which characterized the popular conception of primitivism and natural man.[10] Like all eighteenth-century literary currents, this tradition found easy acceptance in America. The idea of primitivism particularly encouraged American writers to look to the Indian as a source of a legendary American past in much the same way as English poets like Gray and Collins were exploiting the Druids and the Celts.[11] Moreover, American writers, in refuting European charges that the Indian was inferior physically and mentally, exaggerated his good qualities and enforced the tendency to idealize him.

---

[9] See Jones, *O Strange New World*, 16-20 and 42-61.
[10] Hoxie Neale Fairchild, *The Noble Savage* (New York, 1928), 41-42. See Lois Whitney, *Primitivism and the Idea of Progress in English Popular Literature in the Eighteenth Century* (Baltimore, 1934), Chapter IV for a fuller account of the English idealization of the American Indian. One of the leaders of the war against the American settlers, Mohawk Chief Joseph Brant, was the social lion of London on several occasions and a friend of James Boswell's.
[11] See G. Harrison Orians, "The Rise of Romanticism", *Transitions in American Literary History*, 192-193, for a brief statement of the effect of antiquarianism on American literature after 1815.

On the other hand, the Indian had menaced colonization in North America from the time of Raleigh's first colony on Roanoke Island. John Smith's *General History* (1624), Increase Mather's *A Brief History of the War with the Indians in New England* (1676) and many other treatises chronicled the brutality which God had inflicted on the colonies in the person of the red man. The extensive role played by the Indian in the French and Indian War and on the British side during the Revolution made him a continuing threat in the eighteenth century. In the 1780's and 1790's Indian wars raged on the frontier, encouraged in part by the British and by the American government's habit of ignoring Indian territorial rights. The defeat of the expeditions of Harmer and St. Clair in 1790 and 1791 again showed Americans that the Indian was far from eliminated as an obstacle to frontier expansion.[12]

The atrocities of the Indian wars were exaggerated by the conventions of the Indian captivity narrative. Roy Harvey Pearce has pointed out that by the 1780's the captivity narrative, which had begun as a realistic account of the experiences of settlers, had degenerated into penny-dreadful sensationalism.[13] The Indian became a device of Gothic terror in the earliest American fiction, a fiendish beast who threatened scalping, torture, and death by fire.

By the time the *Columbian Magazine* was published, the reality of the Indian was distorted by these two conflicting literary traditions into almost unrecognizable opposites. The Indian appears in the *Columbian* simultaneously as a sadistic savage and as the romantic and naturally virtuous legendary inhabitant of the New Eden, a contradictory image which the magazine's readers, writers, and editors either did not perceive or chose to ignore. The image has persisted throughout American popular

[12] Roy Harvey Pearce, *The Savages of America: A Study of the Indian and the Idea of Civilization* (Baltimore, Md., 1953), 55. For another discussion of the literary treatment of the Indian during the early national period see Albert Keiser, *The Indian in American Literature* (New York, 1933), Chapters III and IV.

[13] Roy Harvey Pearce, "The Significance of the Captivity Narrative", *American Literature*, XIX (1947), 9.

culture; it accounts not only for the good and bad Indians in Cooper's novels but for the fact that in the movies and television programs of our own time a single Indian such as Geronimo can be alternately villain and hero.

The *Columbian* printed numerous references to the post-Revolutionary Indian war. Particularly, it complained that the conflict impeded the republic's westward expansion and blocked the use of valuable resources. The "Intelligence" gave a monthly account of the progress of the war, and essays discussed the principal issues involved. For example, "A Description of Bald Eagle Valley' (September 1788) noted that farmers could not take advantage of the rich soil of that west-central Pennsylvania area because isolated farms were an easy prey to Indian raids and that the mining of the rich lead resources of the valley had been discontinued because of the Indian threat. Suggestions for concluding the war ranged from one essayist's statement that, since a sustained offensive against scattered tribes in the woods was impossible, the only logical answer was a peace treaty which would guarantee the Indians access to western hunting grounds (September 1792, p. 184) to another's suggestion that the only means of defeating the Indians was to attack villages and kill women and children until the warriors, out of regard for their families, came to terms (January 1792, pp. 7-8).

Poets of similar sentiment emphasized the Indian's brutality. Excerpts from a poem entitled "The Returned Captive" described the thoughts of an American soldier as he awaited execution in an Indian camp. At the beginning of the poem, the mood is set by the anguish of tortured captives in the background:

> When thro' the grove the flaming fires arise,
> And loud resound the tortur'd pris'ners cries:
> Still as their pains are more or less extreme,
> The bitter groan is heard, or sudden scream:
> But when their natures fail'd and death drew near,
> Their screeches faintly sounded in the ear.
>
> (December 1787, p. 832)

Other poets, such as David Humphreys and the pseudonymous Constantia, mentioned the potential progress of a western territory cleared of the Indian threat but emphasized brutality. Humphreys in "The Genius of America" contrasted the present situation on the frontier, where

> . . . rove the naked tribes embrown'd
>   Who feed on living gore.
> To midnight orgies, off'rings dire,
> The human sacrifice in fire,

to the future happiness of the region when the savages would be driven away by the forces of civilization and progress:

> The peopling hamlets wide extend,
> The harvests spring, the spires ascend,
> Mid greatful songs of peace.
>
> (February 1787, p. 296)

Constantia marvelled that Philadelphia, the cultural center of the New World with its Peale's art gallery, its Theatre where Shakespeare and Garrick were played in all their native force, and a university where men of science like Rittenhouse and Franklin astounded the world, could have sprung up

> Where late the untutor'd savage wildly rov'd,
> And vast Savannas scenes of rapine prov'd,
> Where gloomy tribes, with murderous intent,
> Track'd o'er the soil, on deathful courage bent;
> Where the tremendous song was heard from far,
> And savage whoops proclaim'd destructive war. . . .
>
> (August 1790, p. 121)

She wondered if cultural excellence similar to Philadelphia's might not someday grace the wild frontier.

In the reports of Indian atrocities, the literary traditions of the captivity narrative intermixed with reality and pushed the characterization of the Indian toward even greater brutality. Most of the reports of the Indian wars which appear in the "Intelligence" and elsewhere in the magazine exhibit the stylistic characteristics of the captivity narrative: fast-moving narrative with a minimum of editorial comment, melodramatic appeals to the sensibility of the reader, and copious sensational details of physical torture and the death pangs of the captives. Almost every month the "Intelligence" printed accounts of punitive expeditions, of settlers' scalps found in deserted Indian villages, and of murder and mutilatation. In October and November 1786 the "Intelligence" carried a detailed report of the torture of a Kentucky family whose men were forced to watch while the Shawnees first cut off the legs of the mother and daughter and then burned the two women alive. Many of these incidents were narrated in a simple, unrhetorical style uncommon during the time. The following description from the April 1788 "Intelligence" tells its story with a minimum of elaboration and bombast, depending upon the natural pathos of the events to touch the reader's sensibility:

On the 12th inst. a party of Savages were discovered at the plantation of Mr. Sikes, about a mile on the south side of Williamson's swamp, by the barking of the dogs, about two o'clock in the afternoon. Mr. Sikes went over the fence to see what they were barking at, when he was fired at by a party of Indians, and received three balls in his arm, shoulder and hip; as he was going into his house, he received another shot, which broke his leg; the party also shot at Mrs. Sikes, as she stood at the door. Mr. Sikes, notwithstanding his wounds, now prepared to defend his wife and four children, but the Savages did not attempt the house. A young man from a neighbouring family hearing the report of the guns, came to the house, and finding Mr. Sikes in that situation, went to the fort for assistance; he returned again immediately with one Allen Spurlock, who placed Mr. Sikes on a bed in a sledge, with one of his daughters, about nine years old, his wife's sister, about 16 years old, walking, and Mrs. Sikes on horse-back, with one child before and one behind her, and proceeded toward the fort, (the young man having gone into the swamp to bring off another family;) but before they reached it, they were fired on by the Indians, who had come up in their rear; upon which they all ran and left Mr. Sikes, and in attempting to gain the fort, the young woman and Allen Spurlock were shot and scalped. The little girl, carrying a bottle of rum in her hand, begged the savages to accept it, and to spare her life; but they d - - d her and her rum, and said they wanted her scalp; upon which they knocked her down and scalped her. (p. 233)

Similar in style are extracts from David Humphreys' "Life of General Putnam" (November 1788) which recounted Putnam's captivity during the French and Indian War. Even the anonymous biographer of Pocahontas felt compelled to remind his readers of the barbarity characteristic of the Indian. He included in a long footnote the frequently reprinted story of the torture and murder of members of Col. Crawford's expedition into Ohio in 1782, a work originally published in 1783 for the purpose of convincing readers of the necessity of eliminating those "animals, vulgarly called Indians".[14]

The difficulty in examining such materials lies in separating truth based on the frontiersman's actual experience with the Indians from fiction in the tradition of the captivity narrative.[15] But, whatever the sources, the narrative and poetical material concerning the Indian wars and the torture and murder of white settlers gave the readers of the *Columbian* a picture of the Indian as a bloodthirsty savage who must be tamed or eliminated before the orderly westward expansion of the nation could progress.

Side by side with this view, the *Columbian* printed glorifications of the red man as Noble Savage and defenses against European charges that he was an inferior form of being. Thus the reader of the magazine could find in a single issue Indians butchering women and children and speaking natural wisdom in a naturally poetic style.

The concept of the American Indian as Noble Savage appeared in the *Columbian* chiefly in extracts from Bartram's *Travels* and Jefferson's *Notes on Virginia,* in Charles Thompson's "An Investigation of the Justice of M. Buffon's opinion respecting the Man of America", in a few anonymous poems, and in reviews of Robert Coram's *Political Inquiries* and Mrs. Sarah W. Morton's *Ouabi: or the Virtues of Nature.* These writings characterized the Indian as having a handsome physical appearance, courage, natural wisdom and virtue, oratorical prowess, and a spontaneous life free from the anxieties and vices of civilization.

The physical bearing of the Creek Indians impressed traveller

[14] For an account of this work, which was edited by Hugh Henry Brackenridge, see Pearce, "Significance of the Captivity Narrative", 10.
[15] *Ibid.,* 16-17.

William Bartram, who described one of their chiefs in the following terms:

a tall well made man, very affable and cheerful, about sixty years of age, his eyes lively and full of fire, his countenance manly and placid, yet ferocious, or what we call savage; his nose acquiline, his dress extremely simple, but his head trimmed and ornamented in the true Creek mode. He has been a great warrior, having then attending as slaves, many Yamasee captives, taken by himself when young. (April 1792, p. 259)

Bartram's choice of words, particularly the Roman connotation of the aquiline nose, aimed at an impression of natural nobility and power. Charles Thompson in the March 1788 magazine spoke in similar terms as he refuted Buffon's charges that the red man was physically scrawny, had no beard, and lacked vivacity. To both writers, the Indian's handsome physical appearance indicated that he possessed inherently good characteristics.

Thompson also scoffed at Buffon's charge that the Indian was cowardly, stating that "the unshaken fortitude with which they bear the most excruciating tortures and death, when taken prisoner, ought to exempt them from that character" (p. 136). The anonymous author of "Characteristics of the American Indians" praised not only the Indian's courage but his gentleness and hospitality, saying:

It is a great mistake to think these people are barbarians, always thirsting after human blood. Very different is their character. They are the greatest *peace-lovers*, at the same time that they are, perhaps, the fiercest and boldest *warriors*, on the face of the earth. Their bravery in the day of battle, and their constancy in enduring hardships, have never been excelled by the most renowned *Romans;* nor, in time of peace, have the most generous nations ever outshone them, in acts of humanity, hospitality, justice, and sincerity. (January 1791, p. 18)

But more important than either his handsome appearance or his courage was the Indian's natural wisdom and virtue. Jefferson marvelled at the Indian's talents as an artist, a craftsman, and a thinker, characteristics which proved "the existence of a germ in their minds which only wants cultivation". He believed that nature had given the red man a strong reason and sentiments and a "glowing and elevated" imagination (March 1788, p. 141). Bartram praised the natural wisdom of the Indians which caused their government to be "as little complicated as that which is supposed to direct or rule the approved economy of the ant and bee, and seems to be nothing more than the simple dictates of natural reason" (February 1792, p. 89).

The belief that the Indian possessed natural virtue appealed to the moralist temper of the American character and was perhaps the most commendable quality of the Noble Savage. Bartram stated that the Creek tribes "deserve the encomium of all nations, for their wisdom and virtue in resisting and even repelling" such vices as theft, drunkenness, and marital infidelity (January 1792, p. 8). Mrs. Sarah W. Morton described the virtues of her heroine Azakia in terms so compelling that the *Columbian* reviewer called the passage "truly beautiful" even though he rejected her belief in the Noble Savage:

> No daring vice could e'er control
> Azakia's unpolluted soul.
> Born amidst virtues favor'd race,
> Her mind as faultless as her face,
> Vain must each daring effort prove,
> That uncorrupted breast to move;
> For on the pure translucent stream
> In vain the midnight lightnings beam;
> It lifts its bosom to the day,
> Unsullied as a solar ray.

Mrs. Morton considered nature itself the source of her heroine's virtue, a virtue which extended to every member of her tribe and to all mankind living in similar harmony with nature. Paradoxically, she considered the cultivation of a tender moral sensibility, a civilized virtue, to be the rationale for a life amid the scenes of nature. Such a life gave man every advantage:

> Native Reason's piercing eye,
> Melting Pity's tender sigh,
> Changeless Virtue's living flame,
> Meek Contintement, free from blame,

Open Friendship's gen'rous care,
Ev'ry boon of life is here!

(February 1791, pp. 106-107)

Statements in the *Columbian* concerning the Indian's oratorical powers vindicate the rhetoric of Cooper's Indians. Even writers who took a realistic view of the Indian's savagery and barbarity commended his ability as a speaker. The magazine printed a number of translations of Indian orations and praised all of them highly: one translator even apologized for his inability to do justice to Indian eloquence (October 1788, p. 578).

Two analogies glorified Indian rhetoric. One compared it to the bardic tradition as it appeared in such poems as Gray's "The Bard"; the other found a precedent in classical Rome and Greece. The *Columbian* editor pronounced "A Speech against the Immoderate Use of Spiritous Liquors, delivered by a Creek-Indian" "far superior to any thing of the kind among the moderns; nor will it suffer from a comparison with the best rhetorical compositions of the ancients" (June 1790, p. 367). The anonymous author of "Indian Oratory" in December 1790 believed that the speech of one Mohawk chief "might become the mouth of a *Cato*" and went on to describe in detail the technique and genius of Indian rhetoric:

They shew a very great vivacity and sprightliness of imagination in their haranguing. Their action seems to us something vehement, but we can see that it corresponds exactly to the several passions. Tho' their language has but few roots, yet they render it copious, and extremely fit for oratory, by varrying, compounding, and decompounding their words, and by having constant recourse to metaphors, etc. after the eastern manner. By the frequent use of guturrals, their language is also very sonorous and masculine. Nevertheless, they are extremely nice in their turns of expression, and few, of their best orators, are so far masters of their language, as never to offend the ears of an *Indian* audience. Such a fine ear the people of *Athens* once had, when Demosthenes and Aeschines melted them with rival periods. (December 1790, p. 367)

Several poets, most persistently Joseph Smith of Burlington, New Jersey, tried to imitate the style of Indian oratory in verse, but their efforts were more Ossianic than Indian. Smith's two "Indian Eclogues", which may have been influenced by Thomas Chatterton's "African Eclogues" idealizing the Noble Savage,[16] are love laments spoken by a Mingo warrior. But Smith's taste failed, and his attempt to combine American images and Ossianic rhetoric are unfortunately ludicrous. For example, one of his "Eclogues" begins in high style:

> Scarce had the morn her orient course begun,
> Or early breezes fann'd the rising sun,
> When Mingo on Ohio's margin stood,
> And told his sorrows to the gliding flood. . . .

to be followed ten lines later by this grotesquely humorous description of the warrior's lady love:

> Enraptured while I view her yellow neck,
> As soft as bear-grease, and as beaver sleek,
> From her grey eyes the living lightnings rush,
> Like the fresh dew-drops glitt'ring thro' a bush.

An even more electrifying lapse of taste occurs several lines later when Mingo describes the vain efforts of another squaw to win his love:

> In vain, with gifts of fish, Agolla strove
> To shake my constancy and win my love,
> Her rough advances like a skunk I shun.
>   (November 1786, pp. 146-147)

Few passages in American writing illustrate so completely the utter failure of some authors to reconcile American subject matter and neoclassical form. But the white man's failure to imitate Indian rhetoric did not damage the respect which *Columbian* contributors felt for the red man's natural talents as an orator. Had Cooper's early critics been aware of the extent of this respect, they might have tempered their condemnation of the rhetoric of his Indians.

---

[16] Fairchild, *The Noble Savage*, 472 describes Chatterton's Eclogues. I may be stretching the point here by arguing for an early acquaintance with Chatterton in America.

Perhaps the most important feature of the Indian's identity as Noble Savage was that he lived a spontaneous life free from the debilitating inhibitions of civilization. *Columbian* contributors commented that the Indian's sex life escaped the artificiality and frustration of civilized races. Charles Thompson denied Buffon's charges that the Indian's organs of generation were smaller than the European's and that he had no passion for women, pointing out that the Indian was trained for war and would be disgraced to show an interest in women before he had proven himself as a warrior or to follow the European practice of violating women prisoners. Thompson asserted that the warrior's love life was both spontaneous and consonant and that the civilized passions of jealousy and adultery were totally absent from savage life (March 1788, pp. 135-137).

An anonymous poem "To Amelia" pointed out that the Indian was free from the anxieties produced by worldly ambition and by philosophical speculation. The poet contrasted the misery of modern man to the happy savage,

> . . . who, all wild, untaught,
> Proves not the mental misery of thought;
> His utmost wish to triumph in the course;
> His noblest glory in corporeal force;
> On haply mounting fame's ensanguin'd car,
> He rolls the terrors of sucessful war;
> Enough that thro' th' admiring tribes around,
> His name and actions, transcient meed, resound,
> Nor covets to transmit his well-earn'd praise,
> To rising heroes on succeeding days;
> Contended that one pang alike shall close
> The period of his triumph and his woes;
> Blest that, 'mid present joys, he does not bear
> That painful prescience of a future care:
> Boasting the sweet refinements not to know,
> By which our pleasures sublimated flow.
>
> (November 1786, p. 146)

Such a longing after the carefree life of the Noble Savage sprang from a strongly romantic view of the American Indian, although it is romanticism expressed in neoclassical form. It also moves far from the reality of the Indian's life. Just as the conventions of the captivity narrative drove writers to an exaggeration of the Indian's cruelty for emotional effect, so the myth of the Noble Savage caused American writers to distort their subject in the quest for a super-virtuous native son.

Judging from the frequency of its appearance in the magazine, primitivism and the Noble Savage greatly appealed to the readers of the *Columbian*. However, the editors and reviewers opposed all attempts to glorify the Indian. One of the most serious criticisms of Bartram's *Travels* was that "he magnifies the virtues of the Indians, and views their vices through too friendly a medium" (April 1792, p. 266). Answering Robert Coram's praise of the happiness of savage life, the reviewer suggested that Coram had the power to leave the corruption of civilization and live among the savages, and he recommended that Coram and his followers do so rather than publishing their lies to the world and "still continuing [to live] in that society of which they give such a hideous picture" (February 1791, p. 110). The reviewer of Mrs. Morton's *Ouabi* condemned the poetess for her "highly coloured" view of the virtues and vices of savage life:

... at first view there is something in them which powerfully excites our admiration. Undaunted courage, ardent patriotism, hospitality to strangers, gratitude to friends, respect to the heroes of their nation, and conjugal fidelity, form an exceedingly interesting picture. The absence of an host of vices resulting from society renders this still more attractive. A vivid imagination will readily add to this, until we at length conceive the poetical descriptions of the golden age to be realized. ... But upon a nearer investigation, we are mortified to find, that the picture has enchanted us only from its distance, and from the obscure light in which we had viewed it. We then discover, that most of the good qualities which had excited our admiration, are produced from the situation in which this people is placed; and that which appeared to us virtue is often times the effect of apathy. If the vices of civilized life are absent, its virtues are equally unknown. Revenge, cruelty, treachery, indolence, drunkeness, and a long catalogue of black vices, convince us that the perfection of this state existed only in our imagination; and that a civil government, with all its ills and inconveniences, is still infinitely preferable to the savage state. (February 1791, pp. 105-106)

In order to counteract the impression given by romantic poetry, the editors printed copious extracts from William Morrell's seventeenth-century picture of the savage living amid nature. Although he described the same scenes and men as the writers of the next century, Morrell gave a contrasting idea of the Indian character:

> Those well seene Natiues in graue Nature's hetts,
> All close designes conceale in their deepe breasts:
> What strange attempts so ere they doe intend,
> Are fairly vsherd in, till their last end. . . .
> No former friendship they in minde retaine,
> If you offend once, or your loue detaine:
> They're wondrous cruell, strangely base and vile,
> Quickly displeased, and hardly reconcild.
>
> (September 1788, p. 535)

To the editors of the *Columbian* the hope of the new world was to civilize the Indian and put him to useful purposes rather than to follow him into savagery. The author of the "Tour of the Eastern States", in describing the Nantucket whaling industry, commented on the usefulness of the Indian as harpooner, for he had good eyes and "peculiar alertness and intrepidity in attacking whales. . . ." Jeremy Belknap asserted that the Indian had already been useful to civilization, since his trails made the best possible routes for new roads (November 1792, p. 328). One optimistic poet even looked forward to the day when the Indian would be tamed and put to the work of building the prosperity of the new nation:

> E'en the fierce Indian shall confess,
> That industry can truly bless;
> That hand, the tomahawk which wields,
> Shall guide the plow o'er fertile fields,
> And, owning civilization's aid,
> Bid the strong mansion rear its head.
>
> (June 1791, p. 411)

Other writers used the Indian as the basis of a legendary American past by postulating the theory that he was descended from civilized peoples. Captain Isaac Stuart of the South Carolina cavalry described a tribe living along the Red River who had white skin, red hair, and spoke a language similar to Welsh. He also reported a legend current with these people that they had migrated to West Florida across the sea many years before the first Spanish explorers came. Stuart thus concluded that the Indians might not be savages at all but descendants of earlier Celtic explorers, a suggestion which paralleled the popular British literary use of Celtic antiquity (March 1787, pp. 318-320).

The *Columbian* contributed several items to the sizable body of literature asserting that the Indians were one of the Ten Lost Tribes of Israel. To prove the identity of the Indians and the Jews, an extract from Beattie's *Journal in America* cited many common customs and beliefs such as the separation of women at first menstruation, the practice of circumcision, the veneration of prophets or medicine men, a feast similar to the Passover, similar legends of the flood and ark, similar concepts of heaven and hell, a story of flight from oppression through divinely parted waters, and a fierce love of liberty (February 1788, pp. 90-93). An extract from Du Pratz' *History of Louisiana* related a number of Indian folktales analogous to Jewish legends (May 1788, pp. 240-242). The revivalist movement from 1815 to 1840 capitalized on this explanation in order to find the Indian a place in the Christian world; [17] but the editors of the *Columbian* used it to counteract the theory of the Noble Savage by suggesting that the Indian's virtues came from his identity with Biblical peoples, not from his primitivism.

The editors found an unexpected literary value in Indian folklore. A number of pieces in the *Columbian* related myths and traditions taken from Indian oral legends. One of the better of these was the "Origin of the Island of Nantucket" in the July 1787 *Columbian*.[18] According to the story, the god Manship

[17]   Pearce, *The Savages of America*, 61-62, discusses the attempt to connect the Indians and the Ten Lost Tribes. Their connection with the Welsh is explored by David Williams, "John Evans' Strange Journey", *American Historical Review*, LIX (1949), 277-295, 508-529.

[18]   I find no record of this tale in Stith Thompson, *Motif-Index of folk-literature* nor in the standard collections of American Indian folk tales. Either it is uncollected or it was authored by a *Columbian* contributor. Since it was probably contributed by Jeremy Belknap, whose writings are usually factual and reliable ,the tale is probably authentic.

once lived on the west end of Martha's Vineyard and boiled whales in a volcano there to feed the Indians. Once, to show their gratitude, the Indians gave him all the tobacco grown during a single season, with which the god filled his pipe. When he finished smoking, he "turned out the ashes of it into the sea, which formed the island of Nantucket". Such legends were made more acceptable to the early national period by one writer's assertion that the republican form of government common to most American Indian tribes was responsible for their natural eloquence and imagination and prefigured a potential development of the same talents in American civilization (December 1790, p. 367).

Judged on the basis of the literature in the *Columbian*, the Indian was perhaps the most usable American theme to the writers of the early national period because he fitted already established literary conventions. The sadistic sensationalism of the captivity narrative was one of the few native American literary traditions, and the concept of the Noble Savage imported from Europe became more and more palatable to Americans as the Indian was driven deeper into the forest. The red man provided legendary associations for the poet and romancer and villainous terror for the Gothic and sentimental novelist. The Noble Savages of Bryant and Longfellow differ little from their ancestors in the *Columbian*, and Robert Montgomery Bird in *Nick of the Woods* still regarded the Indian as a beast to be eliminated by the tide of progress. Although the uniting of the two views into a tragic portrayal of the vanishing American had to wait for James Fenimore Cooper, the ingredients with which he worked were fully developed in the *Columbian* in the 1780's and 1790's.

3. THE PAST

The search for a usable past consumed much of the literary energy of the early national period. Nationalistic fervor demanded that history be used to figure the political, social, and moral glory of the present. Classical literature was the inevitable model for such an achievement; an American *Aeneid*, the ideal. Poets, novelists, and essayists sought in the American past a *mythos* to guide present and future generations.

The colonial past resisted such a mythic metamorphosis. As Benjamin T. Spencer has pointed out, colonial times were "thin in imaginative associations and the aboriginal past culturally alien" to the post-Revolutionary author.[19] Not until Irving discovered the satiric potential of Dutch New York and Hawthorne the psychological and spiritual possibilities of Puritan New England did the colonial past become an organic part of our literary heritage. In the 1780's and 1790's the conventions of genre limited the uses of historical material and closed a large area of native subject matter to literature.

What interest in colonial times did exist was antiquarian and anthropological rather than literary. Indian mounds and other signs of a prehistoric aboriginal society provided material for a number of historical and geographical essays, but no belletristic use was made of them. The poetic uses of the early American past were almost entirely restricted to a few references to Columbus and to the discovery of America as an act of Providence for the rejuvenation of mankind. A few poems such as the "Ode Sung at the Great Wigwam of the Tammany Society" (October 1792, p. 264) approach an Adamic interpretation of American destiny, but fall short of its fullest development in the Manifest Destiny philosophy.

The most appealing use of colonial history to the readers of the *Columbian* was apparently the list of antique laws and curious customs. A few authors tried to trace the spirit of freedom back to colonial ancestors. Several articles emphasized the fact that the early settlers of New England and Pennsylvania fled from civil and religious persecution to establish tolerant and democratic governments on American soil, and one wag defended the democracy of bundling.[20] But for the most part laws and customs were listed for their intrinsic interest alone.

---

[19]   Spencer, *The Quest for Nationality*, 16.
[20]   Jeremy Belknap insisted that William Penn's early government of Pennsylvania adumbrated American democracy; see his "Life of William

The most extensive literary use of the colonial past was Jeremy Belknap's allegory *The Foresters*, which began with the conflict between John Bull and his neighbors Nic Frog and Louis over a tract of land and included allegorical treatments of the Plymouth colonization, New England religious controversy, and colonial policies leading up to the Revolution. Belknap's treatment was often satirical, as was his biting criticism of the white man's manipulation of the red to suit his own purposes (October 1787, pp. 708-709). The *Columbian* continued to serialize Belknap's popular allegory for almost a year, but no other writer attempted a similar imaginative use of colonial history.

The Revolution, on the other hand, provided the epic scope and the tragic sublimity suited to the myth of American greatness. Like the Greeks before the walls of Troy or Aeneas at the Tiber, Americans had forged their national destiny in the fire of epic conflict. God had manifested his Providence in the American victory and, in so doing, had given American writers the seeds of a national mythology based not on shadowy legends but on living realities. Washington and Franklin became national heroes equal to the greatest of classical antiquity or modern times. And the Revolution itself provided a subject not only epic in its grandeur but uniquely American.[21]

That spirit of hero-worship which has caused Americans to elect a military hero President after all but one American war, allied with the venerated epic tradition, led writers to create heroes and demigods of the men prominent during the Revolution. Epics, odes, and eulogistic character sketches featured

Penn" which ran in the *Columbian* from April through September 1789. The anonymous defender of bundling said: "When America shall erect societies for the promotion of chastity in Europe, ... then Europe will discover that there is more Christian philosophy in American *bundling*, than can be found in the customs of nations more polite." (October 1788, 561.)

[21] Professor Spencer has noted: "It not only contained novel scenes and episodes to which transatlantic authors could lay no claim; it also involved inclusive principles which might well re-enforce epic or tragic sublimity. From the Revolution, indeed, one might glimpse Divinity itself. ... " *The Quest for Nationality*, 42.

Washington, Franklin, Adams, and a host of lesser heroes. Some poems merely catalogued those who "deathless praise have won!"

> Bold *Adams*, – gentler *Dickinson*, –
> *Hancock's* determin'd soul, combin'd
> With *Jefferson's* enlightened mind . . .
> To *Gates* immortal praise be given,
> Whilst *Warren's* spirit rests in Heaven.
>
> (October 1790, p. 265)

A popular literary game was the "Enigmatic List of Some of the Patriotic Sons of Columbia, who gloriously signalized themselves in the late happy Revolution", in which the author often strained his wit to the breaking point so his readers could puzzle over the identity of such figures as "A titular saint, two-sevenths of a soldier, to be conspicuous (omitting a letter), a consonant, a preposition, and a half a negative" (December 1789, p. 696).[22] The mere names of heroes were expected to fill the American breast with pride.

George Washington was the supreme legendary hero of the Revolution. By the time the *Columbian* was printed, he was rapidly being apotheosized into a mythic figure.[23] His heroism, his military genius, and his modest retirement to Mount Vernon at the war's end provided themes for poets and orators. Legends sprang up concerning Mount Vernon and his associates. An "Anecdote" in the *Columbian* for March 1788 told of a British frigate's threat to Mount Vernon and of Mr. Lund Washington's defiance of the British, an act which so impressed the British captain that he spared the house.

[22]   George Washington. George is the titular saint, "Wa" two-sevenths of a warrior, "shin" shine omitting a letter, *g* to consonant, *to* the preposition and *n* half of no. The same game was played with Benjamin Franklin and several other Revolutionary heroes.

[23]   William Alfred Bryan, *George Washington in American Literature 1775-1865* (New York, 1952), discusses the literary treatment of Washington by his contemporaries. However, Bryan overlooks the considerable amount of Washington material in the *Columbian* and, except for one brief mention (p. 53), seems unaware of the efforts to make Washington a mythological figure during his own lifetime.

Writers considered the perpetual endurance of the Washington legend certain. One envisioned a future time when a barbarian ignorant of history might break a statue of Washington; but "when from the ruins of the inscription they shall collect the name of Washington, the chief of these Barbarians or savages, instructed by tradition of the American revolution, will be avenged for the outrageous attempt, and cause the monument to be repaired" (January 1787, p. 227). Although the Washington legend was created largely after his death, even before and during his presidency the *Columbian* was praising his greatness and comparing him to the most acclaimed figures of classical antiquity.

Washington gave Americans and the world an example of modest patriotism. "Patriotism: An Ode" claimed that:

> Of those, who oft their courage tried;
> Who noble liv'd or nobly died,
> *Good Washington* we own supreme,
> The *soldier's* pride and the *patriot's* theme.
>
> (October 1790, p. 265)

One writer remarked that most men become heroes out of vanity, but Americans "have been actuated by a love of their country, by a love of liberty! Yes – we can give a recent instance in the illustrious WASHINGTON" (February 1789, p. 99). But however great his military prowess, his modest retirement to Mount Vernon at the end of the war shone even brighter. One anonymous poet named Washington as "One rare example" in all the history of military conquerors, for he withdrew to private life rather than making himself a dictator:

> Tis Washington retir'd to life's still scene,
> Whose claim, like Caesar's legion cou'd sustain;
> Whom boundless trust ne'er tempted to betray,
> Nor power impell'd to arbitrary sway.
> Such Washington, his rescu'd country's theme,
> Columbia's glory, 'minish'd Britain's shame.
> Too weak the muse, th' illustrious chief to sing
> A private citizen, who might be king.
>
> (November 1787, p. 781)

A. J. Dallas's "Address intended to have been spoken by Mr. Hallam at the Theatre, in Philadelphia, on the 4th of July, 1788" alluded to the nation's pride when Washington chose to return to rural life:

> The patriot bosom glows *as he retires;*
> While all mankind, in admiration lost,
> Strive who can follow or applaud him most.
>
> (July 1788, p. 407)

James Tilton went so far as to say that it was only in obedience to the voice of God that the modest leader agreed to accept his election as first President of the United States.

The *Columbian* printed detailed accounts of the public's adoration of its hero. Throughout his journey from New York to Philadelphia after being inaugurated President, he was greeted in every village by triumphant arches and poetical recitations.[24] In their "Account of the Manner of receiving at Trenton, his Excellency GEORGE WASHINGTON", the *Columbian* editors described how, "as he entered the town, the women and children, who lined the streets dressed in white, sang the following sonata:"

> Welcome, mighty chief! once more
> Welcome to this grateful shore:
> Now no mercenary foe
> Aims again the hostile blow –
> Aims at thee the fatal blow.
> Virgins fair, and matrons grave,
> These thy conqu'ring arms did save.
> They for thee triumphant bow'rs
> Build, and strew thy way with flow'rs   –
>
> (May 1789, p. 289)

The same issue reported a similar reception at Gray's Ferry in Pennsylvania.

---

[24] After his election, Washington journeyed from Mount Vernon to New York for the inauguration. All along his route he was greeted with great pomp and ceremony. Particularly impressive were the receptions at Alexandria, Georgetown, Philadelphia, Trenton, New Brunswick, and New York. These incidents are described in detail in Edward C. Towne's revision of Schroeder-Lossing, *Life and Times of Washington* (Albany, N. Y., 1903), 1594-1600.

It is not surprising that, in attempting to create a national hero, poets mythologized. Francis Hopkinson's "Musical Entertainment" the "Temple of Minerva" (April 1787) concluded the triumphant entry of the conquering hero with a passage of rhapsodic praise in which Washington was metaphorically deified as the son of the goddess Columbia. Even a mythical *jeu d'esprit* entitled "The Life and Adventures of Jack Frost" exploited the popularity of the national hero: Jack Frost's activities in America included the following –

> When WASHINGTON's genius impell'd him to turn
> On the foe who had chas'd him with pride and with scorn,
> I lent him my snow and my ice and my hail,
> And TRENTON beheld how his troops did prevail.
>
> (February 1788, p. 110)

A favorite mythological technique was to compare Washington to the greats of classical antiquity. The epithet "The American FABIUS" became early attached to him and was frequently used in historical as well as belletristic writings in the *Columbian*.[25] The comparison ranged to other classical and modern heroes. In the eulogistic "Portrait of General Washington" the author comments:

Like Camillus he forsook the charms of rural life and flew to the assistance of his country; like Fabius he saved it by procrastinating; like Peter the great he triumphed over his enemies by experiences acquired by misfortune. There is not a man, not a monarch in Europe who would not envy the glory of having acted such a part as Washington. (January 1787, p. 228)

In July 1790 the *Columbian* printed a poetical recitation delivered at the commencement of the University of Pennsylvania in which American heroes were substituted for the worthies of antiquity. Washington played a prominent part.

> For CINCINNATUS, see a WASHINGTON!
> Alike amid the storms of WAR renown'd,
> In PEACE with a superior glory crown'd;

[25] See, for example, January 1787, 228; February 1789, 128; and August 1792, 140.

Not thron'd in the proud pageantry of state,
But in the bosoms of the good and great;
The firm avenger of his country's cause
Guardian of JUSTICE, LIBERTY and LAWS!

(p. 56)

Emelia's poem "Addressed to General Washington" carried the identification of Washington with heroes and demigods to even greater extremes. She began by evoking Washington as the muse of her song and continued to suggest the epic proportions of his greatness by declaring him superior to Virgil's hero:

Not good Aeneas who his father bore,
And all his household gods from ruin'd Troy,
Was more the founder of the Latian realm,
Than *thou* the basis of this mighty fabric,
Now rising to my view, of arms, of arts;
The seat of glory in the western world.

(January 1787, p. 245)

The elevation of Washington into a mythical figure was easy because of the parallels between his career and those of classical heroes Fabius, Cincinnatus, and Camillus. His military genius in winning American independence and his modest retirement into private life symbolized to American writers the best qualities of a democratic society, and he was made its representative man. Moreover, the literary tradition which American writers knew best suggested to them that America's heroes must somehow fit into epic patterns worthy of Greece and Rome.[26] Therefore, they developed by association a rhetorical myth of Washington's classical greatness just as Mason Locke Weems was later to weave a myth of his common sense virtue.

Next to Washington, the most venerated American was Benjamin Franklin. During the time the *Columbian* was published, Franklin was known internationally as a patriot, scientist, statesman, and man of letters. Although he was not mythologized to the degree of Washington, he did provide an example of the

[26] For a discussion of the considerable influence of Rome on American culture see Jones, *O Strange New World*, Chapter VII.

versatility and greatness possible in a democratic environment.

Franklin was revered as the patriarch of the American continent whose accomplishments equalled those of any man, living or dead. As one poet phrased it:

> Patriot! philosopher! and sage!
> Immortal be thy name!
> Virtue shall spread thy worth through every age,
> And wisdom celebrate thy fame.
> In council wise, firm in debate,
> Thy virtues oft preserved each state;
> These states acknowledged flourishing and free,
> Shall yield the palm of genius still to thee.
>
> (June 1791, p. 409)

Moreover, his achievements placed him on the level of the great names of history. One poet predicted that "Franklin soon (for who can fate decry?) / With Bacon in conjecture's paths may vie" (August 1791, p. 126). William Smith in his "Eulogium on Benjamin Franklin" stated that "*Franklin*, as a philosopher, might have become a *Newton*; as a lawyer, a *Lycurgus*: but he was greater than either of them, by uniting the talents of both, in the practical philosophy of doing good . . ." (May 1792, p. 324). A 1790 University of Pennsylvania commencement poem characterized Franklin as Newton's superior; the gods gave Newton only half-truths and reserved for Franklin the inner secrets of science:

> Last NEWTON rose – and, borne on eagle-wings,
> Collected knowledge from a thousand springs,
> Bound down the planets in the blue expanse,
> And would have pierc'd all NATURE at a glance,
> Had not the Goddess, in her dread decree,
> Reserved, for FRANKLIN's hand, the golden key,
> That opes her inmost doors – O last and best
> Of *Patriots* and *Philosophers* confess'd,
> Whose ever-working comprehensive mind
> Labour'd love to benefit mankind!
> All-hail COLUMBIA, to your favourite son!
> All-hail, these happy walls! your FOUNDER own!
> With grateful strains, ye *Sons of Science* Come!
>
> (July 1790, p. 52)

Franklin's electrical experiments seemed particularly impressive to American writers. Henry Stuber praised Franklin's scientific mind, his utilitarian motives, and his most important discovery: "Animated with the true Newtonian spirit of philosophising; . . . he dived into the hidden recesses of nature, and developed some of her most important secrets. . . . Utility was constantly his aim." His discovery of the lightning rod was "a lasting monument to his ingenuity and success" (May 1790, p. 269). An anonymous poet praised Dr. Franklin for daring "to chain / The thunder's flash, and half its rage restrain . . ." (September 1790, p. 186). William Smith pointed out that Franklin was the first to draw lightning from the sky by artificial means and predicted that that discovery alone would suffice to insure Franklin's everlasting fame (May 1792, p. 324).

Writers also venerated Franklin for his role in winning American independence. Stuber pointed out that love for his country was Franklin's earliest passion and that the latter part of his life was inexorably entwined with the history of the Revolution (May 1790, p. 269). An Irish poet praised Franklin's patriotism and hoped that his example would be an incentive for Irish independence (July 1787, p. 560). William Smith praised Franklin's diplomatic achievements and quoted a letter from Jefferson which described the great respect the French nobility and populace felt for Franklin (May 1792, pp. 324-325). A poem entitled "Patriotism; an Ode" found a place for Franklin's diplomacy among the gods: "*Franklin*, in France who mildly shone, / Prov'd, both *Minerva's* are our own" (October 1790, p. 265).

Partially, no doubt, because he was a Philadelphian, but chiefly because he illustrated the greatness possible for an American, the *Columbian* printed a large body of Franklin material, including praise from foreign publications; and, although the reviewer of Smith's "Eulogium" believed that Smith's examination of Franklin's religious principles should have been omitted lest the gullible be led into believing their hero an agnostic, most of the comments helped build a heroic legend around the man. The *Columbian* particularly valued Lord Kames's remark that Franklin was "a man who makes a great figure in the learned world; and who would still make a greater figure for benevolence and candour, were virtue as much regarded in this declining age as knowledge" (Supplement III, p. 775).

In comparison to Franklin and Washington, other heroes seemed mundane and dull. Military leaders Charles Lee, Nathaniel Greene, and Joseph Warren received the thanks of several writers, but none were elevated into myths. Philadelphia lawyer Able James was praised for his support of "the patriotic FRANKLIN in public spirited opposition to Proprietory and Parliamentary encroachments" on American freedom (November 1790, pp. 287-288); but the association with Franklin is obviously more important than James's own achievements. Governor William Livingston of New Jersey received perhaps the highest praise possible for an American in an anonymous elegy in September 1790 where he was described as "Second in fame alone to *Washington*" (p. 187).

One interesting attempt to create a heroic legend was David Humphreys' "Life of General Putnam" (October and November 1788), which Leon Howard has called the precursor of the Parson Weems mythical biography.[27] Humphreys' work resembles fiction more than biography. At his hand Putnam becomes a proto-Leatherstocking. An episode in which Putnam crawls headfirst into a narrow den to kill a marauding she-wolf and a long passage describing Putnam's fight with an Indian at Ticonderoga and his subsequent capture and escape use American material for gothic effect with a skill not equalled until Charles Brockden Brown's *Edgar Huntley*.

The only other American compared to European greats was former *Columbian* editor Francis Hopkinson. At the time of Hopkinson's death in 1791 a poet who signed himself "W" described Hopkinson as:

> *A Sage expired!* – who prized the rights of man,
> And blended nature's claims with wisdom's plan.
> The steady foe of tyranny confess'd,
> He by true *wit* licentiousness suppressed.

> (May 1791, p. 338)

[27] Leon Howard, *The Connecticut Wits*, 245.

In the same issue Benjamin Rush compared Hopkinson to Lucian, Swift, and Rabelais and said that "for wit, humour, and good sense" his "A Pretty Story" would "last as long as the citizens of America continue to admire, and to be happy under, the present national government of the United States".

More interesting, perhaps, than the treatment of Hopkinson in the *Columbian* is the omission of Philip Freneau and Thomas Paine from the list of Revolutionary literary heroes. From October 1791 until the death of the *Columbian* in 1792, Freneau lived in Philadelphia and edited Jefferson's controversial *National Gazette*. Since the *Columbian* eschewed political involvement, it naturally avoided praising a writer so closely connected with one of the contending political factions of the time. Paine, during this period, was assailing the monarchies of England and France with his book *The Rights of Man*. Although the *Columbian* printed extracts from the book and his letters to his friend Benjamin Rush, no reference to Paine's contribution to the Revolution appeared, perhaps because his close alliance with French radicals caused conservative Pennsylvania Federalists to consider him a dangerous Jacobin. Apparently, even before the publication of *The Age of Reason*, Paine's reputation in Philadelphia had suffered a decline.

Not only did the Revolution give the nation its heroes, it was a subject of intrinsic interest to American readers. The editors of the *Columbian* felt obliged to provide their readers a comprehensive treatment of its history and effect. They devoted a large percentage of space to the serialized "History of the Revolution" and attacked such abbreviated summaries as Noah Webster's in *Fugitiv Essays* as "too concise":

Abridgements of ancient history may frequently be useful and proper; but surely no man who wishes for information, on a subject of so much importance, as the revolution which gave freedom and national existence, to this great empire, will be satisfied with the perusal of these sketches, comprized in *fifty* pages. (October 1790, p. 254)

Instead, they recommended full treatments such as David Ramsay's *History of the Revolution of South-Carolina* which, they believed, would lay the groundwork for future American literature.

Most writers did not wait for the future; they adapted the Revolution to the genres and theories of the present. A common use of the Revolution was as the background for sentimental tales. Since, most writers believed, sensibility operated on the principles of associational psychology, the names Saratoga, Monmouth, Trenton, Valley Forge, and King's Mountain instantly aroused the reader's pride and patriotism; and the association of a character with one or more of these battles automatically surrounded him with an aura of heroism. In addition, the Revolution provided novelists a new set of complications to frustrate ambitions and part lovers. Handsome British officers seduced the heroines of "Amelia; or the Faithless Briton" and "The History of Leander and Matilda", who were unable to see the homespun virtues of their American suitors. The parting of lovers gave authors the opportunity to exercise their rhetoric and to exhibit the conflict of love and patriotism in the breasts of the hero and heroine. Typical is Arabella's anguish when duty called her lover Altmont to war:

he is summoned to arms – the voice of his country demands his exertions – Foreign domination impends, and unconditional submission is required. He rushes to war. – The tumult of passion swells in the bosom of Arabella. – She utters the involuntary scream – she faints .– ... His heart was divided between love and glory. Love exacted his sighs and anguish; but patriotism, in the breast of the hero, supersedes all other considerations. (November 1790, pp. 308-309)

The gothic novelist emphasized the terrors of the war. In one tale the heroine is scalped by a band of Indians fighting under a British commander and her lover killed taking revenge on the band. In another the hero dies a grisly death in battle.

Poets, too, utilized the Revolution for sentimental effects. "William and Lucy: An American Ballad" tells of a country girl enticed to Philadelphia by a charming city youth, causing her country sweetheart to join the Army in despair (May 1789). Another bit of poetical sentimentalism occurred in "Poetical Epistle written in England by a Young American, in the British Army", which describes the author's joining the British cause and his

subsequent disillusionment with his chosen country. At the end of
the poem he confesses:

> But had I thought insidious Britain meant,
> With hell's dark views, and infamous intent,
> To forge base fetters for oppression's hand,
> The scourge and terror of my native land   –
> By all the sacred host of heav'n, I swear,
> My country's welfare should have been my care,
> To shield her liberty, my daily aim,
> And independence been my road to fame.
>
> (September 1786, p. 42)

The reassurance that those Americans who had followed the
Tory cause were aware of their error and recognized the divine
right of the American rebellion comforted an audience which
was sure it had followed God's path in seeking independence.
The emotional wounds caused by broken families and conflict
among friends could be healed to some extent by such poetical
confessions of the rightness of American independence coming
from an American in the British Army.

The most common literary use of the Revolution occurred in
rhetorical occasional verse celebrating American freedom and
might. Some, such as the "Verses inscribed to Monmouth"
(August 1791, p. 123), attempted to use Revolutionary events to
give the American scene needed emotional and historical associations. The poet assumed that the glory won at Monmouth
would forever endear the ground to Americans and make it
possible for future poets to use Monmouth, much as an English
poet would use Bosworth Field, with the assurance that a multi-
level emotional association would be evoked.

Other poems, like "To the King of England", which originally
appeared in *Common Sense* in 1778, or various Revolutionary
poems by David Humphreys or Francis Hopkinson, were reprinted to maintain the pitch of patriotism achieved during the
war. Most of these poems attempt to play on the reader's sensibility by describing the suffering of American citizens during the
war. "To the King of England" brands George III as a second
Cain, "Alike in cruelty, alike in hate, / In guilt alike, and more

alike in fate." An affecting passage later in the poem describes
the suffering of war orphans but is marred, as were so many
American poems of the time, by an unintentionally humorous
rhyme:

> Why cries the orphan – "Oh my father's slain!"
> Why hangs the sire his paralytic head,
> And nods with manly grief, – "My son is dead!"
> Why shrieks the maiden, (robbed of ease and sense,)
> *"He's gone – He's killed – Oh! Heavens, take me hence."* . . .
> Why lisps the infant on its mother's lap
> And looking round the parlour – "Where is pap".
>
> (February 1791, p. 117)

In this, as in many cases, the combination of American colloquialism and neoclassical rhetoric produced a destructive, incongruous humor.

The *Columbian* printed two essays and one poem which depicted the heroism of American women during the war, although
nothing comparable to the Molly Pitcher legend appeared. "The
Sentiments of an American Woman" (Supplement III, pp. 759-
762) first cited the heroic deeds of the great women of classical
antiquity and then related how American women during the
Revolution sold their fine clothes and ornamental home furnish-
ings to supply clothing for American soldiers. "Female Heroism"
(March 1790, p. 139) described the actions of the ladies of
besieged Charleston who refused to attend social functions at
which British officers were present, preferring instead to care for
American officers in jails and prison ships. The author noted
that "Such exemplary patriotism excited in several British officers
a mean resentment, which put them upon employing the negroes
in rude insults of those distinguished heroines." In December
1789 the magazine printed a song said to have been sung during
the war at a "Spinning frolic", a social gathering at which the
ladies of the region spun clothes for the American troops. The
poem is filled with patriotic sentiments, but ends on the pragmatic
thought that farmers and spinners can only submit to whichever
side wins.

A few writers were able to utilize the exuberant spirit of victory for humorous purposes. In April 1790 the *Columbian* printed a mock oration, "In Praise of Rum" which Mr. George Baynton had delivered at the July commencement of the University of Pennsylvania. One of Baynton's ironic points was that:

RUM is the fuel of courage: of this the British army exhibited many proofs during the late war. ... To this liquor, therefore, we are to ascribe the many gallant exploits, that were performed by the British army in America; such as the burning of Charlestown, New-London, and Norfolk; and, above all, the bravery with which they extirpated old men and women. (pp. 215-216)

"An Original Anecdote" published in April 1789 told of a young American in a London playhouse witnessing an interlude which ridiculed the American Army:

A number of American officers being introduced in tattered uniforms, and bare-foot, the question was put to them severely – What was your *trade* before you enlisted in the army? One answered a *tailor;* another, a *cobbler.* The wit of the piece was to banter them for not keeping themselves cloathed and shod; but before this could be gotten out, the American exclaimed from the gallery, "Great-Britain beaten by tailors and cobblers! huzza!" (p. 255)

In the flush of victory, Americans were able to make their old enemies the butt of the joke.

"Trifler" No. VI found a comic character in the barroom patriot who, although he had not taken part in any battle during the war, in conversation imagines himself the hero of every engagement and "snatches the truncheon from the hand of *General Washington*; and, in regal phraseology, recapitulates the vicissitudes of the war". He portrays himself as "the hero of every triumph and the victim of every wound", sometimes humorously: "*There*, compelled by the inferiority of OUR numbers, to retreat, ... the enemy overtook US, and barbarously refusing quarter, laid every one of US dead upon the field" (March 1788, pp. 139-140).

The Revolution made a curious entrance into the magazine's pages in an article entitled "Merlin's Prophesy of the American Revolution" (June 1787). The author described a book owned by his grandfather in which verses from a 1530 edition of *Merlin's Prophesies* were copied and interpreted as predicting the perpetual endurance of the British Empire. But the author, upon seeing the great seal of the United States, reinterpreted the verses as predicting American independence. For example, in Merlin's fifth prophesy – "The *cock* shall guard the eagle's nest, / The *Stars* shall rise all in the west ..." he saw the eagle as the bald eagle on the arms of the United States, the protecting cock as France, and the rising stars as the rising American empire. This, and six other stanzas, he interpreted in the light of the events of the Revolution and the constitutional convention, proving that God, the Fates, and all other supernatural powers in the universe supported American independence.

The Revolution was a potent American subject because it satisfied two basic urges – the desire for American parallels to classical history and literature and the desire for poetical associations for the American land. Moreover, it was the event of American history most closely associated with the ideology of republicanism, which was the essence of post-Revolutionary nationalism. Few other subjects seemed so pertinent to American life during the early national period.

4. THE AMERICAN CHARACTER

Since they first perceived themselves a nation, Americans have sought to answer Hector St. John de Crevecoeur's question, "What Is an American?" The American land and the socio-political ideology of republicanism, they argued, would obviously transform the human character and create a distinctly American mode of behavior and belief. But what would be the nature of that transformation and in what areas of life would it operate? Contributors to the *Columbian Magazine* offered several tentative answers. Although none of them foresaw the American Character in its full complexity, their comments are interesting as partial, early insights into the direction in which American life would develop in the decades to come.

The magazine's editors and contributors agreed that the new republic had engendered a unique society which was vastly superior to that of the old world. Equality of opportunity had produced optimism, and the simplicity of democratic life had destroyed the awe with which the poor of Europe trembled before their aristocrats. The "Retailer" pointed out that in America only virtue and wisdom brought honor, and those qualities were available to all: "The trappings of the European nations will do little here: the boast of ancient grandeur can never procure modern esteem; . . . our great men owe their greatness to no such things" (October 1789, p. 588). The American would be naturally more virtuous and naturally happier because he lived in a democratic society.

The magazine attacked any suggestion that American life might resemble European. The reviewer of Noah Webster's *Fugitiv Essays* attacked Webster's objection that placing female seminaries in American cities would needlessly expose the girls to vice and temptation by reminding Webster "that the large towns of America, are not, like those in Europe, seats of flagrant vice. The same caution therefore, that may be proper in Great Britain, is by no means so in the United States" (October 1790, p. 254).

At the same time, writers warned American citizens against anything foreign. The infusion of European manners, they feared, might corrupt the natural goodness of American life, and the importation of foreign manufactured goods might destroy the native simplicity of republican society. The *Columbian* denounced any manifestation of the encroachment of European class distinctions and luxuries. Writers urged Americans to be proud of their humble life and to the appellation "Yankee". The "Retailer" pointed out that the Yankee farmer was the backbone of the Revolution and deplored the fact that "these very people who were the first who dared to raise themselves from grinding under oppressing tyranny, to assert their natural claim to liberty, . . . are now regarded with contempt, and instead of its being thought an honor to be sprung from those noble supporters of freedom, it is looked upon as an irreparable disgrace" (March 1788, pp. 151-152). Several writers feared the intrusion of

European titles which would corrupt the egalitarian nature of American life.[28]

Material luxury posed another threat to democracy. The belief that frugality and republicanism went hand in hand was congenial both to the enlightened American common sense of *Poor Richard's Almanack* and to the older Puritan morality. "Pro Republica" feared that American society had already begun to decay, declaring that "we have departed from those plain and simple manners, and that frugal mode of living, which are absolutely indispensible in the infant state of our country, and best suited to our Republican form of government" (December 1786, p. 173). Another writer pointed out that luxurious surroundings, artificial distinctions of rank, and the destruction of democratic institutions inexorably followed one another. After describing the corruption caused in royal courts by the vain flattery of courtiers and the aping of immoral royal manners, he warned: "O ye sons of liberty! ye free-born Americans! let not that bane of domestic happiness, that supporter of luxury, approach the courts of our federal building; let it not exalt the senator above the free citizen, by a self-important dignity, an imitation of patrician pride, the product of vanity" (February 1789, p. 98). Another more economically-oriented writer disparaged foreign luxuries not only because they corrupted the simplicity of American life but because it was un-American to purchase foreign goods. He pointed out that the patriotic citizen would not mind paying a higher price for American goods than for European because he would realize that he was helping advance the material and spiritual growth of his country (February 1787, p. 283).

[28] Russel B. Nye has pointed out that American manners, fashions, and attitudes really changed little after the Revolution. With the exception of the more radical republicans, most American leaders believed in an aristocracy of worth rather than egalitarianism, and England continued to provide the model for American life. (*The Cultural Life of the New Nation*, Chapters 5 and 6.) The more radical statements in the *Columbian* do not indicate that the authors belonged to the extreme political left; they were stimulated by the first flush of victory over the world's leading power and show the enthusiasm with which American writers accepted the implications of national identity.

The contributors to the *Columbian* demanded that American citizens seek and cultivate the peculiarly American. The "Retailer" facetiously insisted that his prose be encouraged because it was of American manufacture. Joseph Cooper demanded that Americans produce a "truly FEDERAL wine", but he was unable to give a recipe or to define what made a wine "federal" (November 1790, p. 325). In November 1788 an article entitled "To the Ladies on the Use of Cosmetics" claimed that the finest cosmetic then in use was a mixture of ground Indian corn and weak lye and proposed that this genuinely American mixture be called "THE FEDERAL COSMETIC". Less ludicrous was Benjamin Rush's demand that American scientists avoid the pedantic Latin jargon of European science and adopt an American terminology. He particularly opposed following Linnaeus's classification of plants and herbs and suggested the use of American names such as "Mohawk-root", "Purple rod", "Ox-weed", and "Poke-weed" (December 1787, pp. 805-807). When they could not find such specific suggestions, American writers simply advanced the general proposition that the Revolution dictated that every phase of American life should conform to the political principles fought for and won on the battlefield.

Writers for the *Columbian* believed that American life had produced a man of unique qualifications and that everything possible should be done to preserve the conditions which make an American. The chief quality of American life they described was unparalleled versatility and adaptability. One essayist described a backwoods Pennsylvania tavernkeeper who claimed: "I am a weaver, a shoemaker, a blacksmith, a wheel-wright, a farmer, a gardner, and upon occasion, a soldier. I bake my bread, brew my own beer, kill my hogs; I built the stable and barn yonder; I shave, bleed, and cure disease" (December 1791, p. 380). The author pointed out that the American farmer generally could make his own house and all his possession without having served an apprenticeship in any trade, could grow his own food, butcher his own meat, and defend his family against attack. How, he asked, could a nation of such self-reliant individuals fail to become the leading power on earth?

The American character, these writers believed, was less the product of the frontier environment of American life than of the democratic government under which Americans lived. Although Benjamin Rush, following Crevecoeur's "What Is an American?" described the three-stage movement of civilization across the continent (November 1786, pp. 117-122), he did not anticipate Frederick Jackson Turner's thesis describing the influence of the frontier on the tone and character of American life. Instead, to Rush, the frontiersman was a curiosity momentarily distracting to the cultured Philadelphian but unconnected with the manner of his life.

Rather, it was a democratic government, which left the individual free to develop in whatever direction he chose, that strengthened the natural abilities of the American character. Like Jefferson, and later Emerson, the writers of the early national period believed that progress was possible only when governmental interference was kept to a minimum.

In order to transfer these republican principles from generation to generation and to insure the survival of the American character, a new mode of education was essential. Benjamin Rush insisted that it was time for America to "study our own character – to examine the age of our country – and to adopt manners in every thing, that shall be accommodated to our state of society, and to the forms of our government" (May 1790, pp. 289-290). He believed it was the duty of the federal government to provide schools which would establish "habits of labour and virtue" among the young and which would bring all of the American people into conformity with "reason, humanity, and the present state of society in America" (August 1790, p. 73).

The education suited to the American situation was intensely pragmatic and utilitarian. An article entitled "Remarks on the Prevalent Mode of Education" insisted that a young man study only the trade he intended to follow. It contended that apprenticeships were much better suited to American society than a university education, that only a merchant needed to know a foreign language, and that "a *liberal education* disqualifies a man for business" (November 1791, p. 315). Education for girls was equally practical. According to one writer, "As the American world is not yet infected with the idleness, dissipation and fastidious delicacy of European manners, the ladies follow the rule of virtue and good sense, and attend to the concerns of their family." Plays and novels were damned for their dubious morality, and only that reading which could impart moral or practical knowledge was recommended (September 1787, p. 644). Benjamin Rush in "On Female Education" (April 1790) remarked that since the American girl married young, she must exclude all but the most practical knowledge from her education. The only liberal study for which she had time was history, and the motive for learning it was to instruct her sons in the "principles of liberty and government". The study of music and foreign languages was not suited "to the present state of society in America" because they took time away from more useful pursuits. Not only laymen concerned with building the nation but professional educators as well excluded humanistic studies from the American curriculum and focused the nation's attention on practical science and engineering. Provost William Smith of the University of Pennsylvania advised his students to "learn to be *useful* citizens":

You did not come into the world to decypher inscriptions on ancient monuments, nor to derive English words from their Greek or Roman originals. – The man who will discover a method of preventing the fly from destroying turnips, or who will point out a new and profitable article of agriculture and commerce, will deserve more from his fellow-citizens and from heaven, than all the Latin or Greek scholars, or all the teachers of technical learning that ever existed, in any age or country. (August 1790, p. 79)

Although this attitude was more common in the middle colonies than in New England, it does indicate the early presence of anti-intellectualism in America and the identification of utilitarian material values with the American way of life.[29] The cultivation

[29] Richard Hofstadter, *Anti-intellectualism in American Life* (New York, 1963), Part 5 traces the distrust of the intellect and the arts in American education from the beginning of the nation to the present day. (For statements relative to the early national period, see pp. 312-316.) Hofstadter attributes this distrust to the emphasis on economic and political practical-

of the mind and the taste was a gentlemanly pursuit, and the gentleman was an aristocratic ornament useless to an egalitarian society.

To theorize about the American character was one thing; to embody it in literature, another. The American character remained elusive to the writer of belles lettres. In only a few rare instances, most of them in periodical essays, were elements of the American character used for literary purposes.

The *Columbian* printed two essays which anticipated western humor, American dialect, and the motif of the Yankee versus the Backwoodsman which one scholar sees as the central myth of our national character and history.[30] One was a reprinting of Reverend Samuel Peters' description of the riot caused in Windham, Connecticut, by the mass migration of frogs to a pond in the area, a story which Constance Rourke calls the precursor of the Western tall tale.[31] The other was a long anecdote in "Retailer" No. X which combined many of the features of the early native American humor.[32]

American humor began with a sense of the rich diversity of American life and the comically incongruous contrast between every American and his fellow countrymen. The humor of the first indigenous character in American drama, Jonathan, the Yankee servant in Royall Tyler's *The Contrast*, was developed by contrasting Jonathan to the foppish, gentlemanly Jessamy. A similar contrast lies at the heart of the Retailer's account of his

---

ity in American life, the same motives expressed by the educational theorists whose writings appeared in the *Columbian*.

[30] Hoffman, *Form and Fable*, Chapter 3, "The American Hero: His Masquerade", traces the development of the frontiersman as the American folk hero, and Chapter 4 discusses Washington Irving's "The Legend of Sleepy Hollow" as the first important literary statement of the conflict between the culturally sophisticated but effete city man (Ichabod Crane) and the crude but effective frontiersman (Brom Bones). Such a conflict, Hoffman believes, is central to the search for the identity of the American character.

[31] *American Humor* (New York, 1931), 37.

[32] The most detailed elaboration of those features is Walter Blair, *Native American Humor* (San Francisco, 1960), 3-37. The framework for my discussion of "Retailer" No. X comes from Blair.

encounter with a Pennsylvania farm family. The Retailer pictures himself as a city gentleman who has frequently joined his fellow Philadelphians in laughing at the ignorance of country bumpkins on the stage. But when he travels twenty-five miles into the Pennsylvania countryside to escape the July heat, he finds that city knowledge is country ignorance. He has never seen a field of rye, thrashes himself rather than the wheat with the flail, confuses a cow and a horse, and finds that city manners make little impression on a country girl.

The Retailer heightened the comedy by juxtaposing his own Addisonian style with the dialect of his hosts. In contrast to his Latinate vocabulary and flowing periods are dialect idioms like "dad rat it", "burn my wig", "needs have", "burn me if you *ever*", and "I vow"; dialect spellings like "galls" and "dont"; and rustic metaphors like "the cow and the hay stack will soon get together". The Retailer climaxes the contrast by asserting his city knowledge:

I had to bluster out in my own defence, "*Tytyre tu patulae recubans*" or I should have been noted as the most ignorant man in the world. "What *for* talk is that", says Sam. "Why Greek", says I, "it means many men of many of minds". Every countenance betrayed that kind of surprize, that would be expressed in the question, can any good thing come out of Nazareth?" an old fellow who was seated in one corner, observed, that it was "a cow for the milk and the horse for the plough"; and that although they were running their *rigs* upon the gentleman, he might make them look foolish yet; O yes says Sam, mr. P. knows Greek, but the *Greek* in his head wont keep the flail from brusing it; neither will Greek learn him how to plough or reap. –

The essay also employed a variation of the common humorous device "the courtin'" which is best known in James Russell Lowell's *Biglow Papers* but which had wide currency in newspapers and magazines in the 1790's and early years of the nineteenth century.[33] The son of his host takes the Retailer to visit some "nation civil galls". He courts them in his best "Phil-delphy" manner, with disastrous results. Later, the farm boy's sisters ask how the slicker behaved with the girls:

[33] See Blair, 24-25.

"Well", says Sammy, "after we got in, I goes and sets by Sal, and begins to handle her a little, and I thought as how I'd let Kitty and *he* make the best of the matter between themselves; but I vow now, and it is not a bit of a lie, he was talking about how the galls in town dressed, and such like things, for two hours, instead of laying hold of her, and giving her a *squeeze* or so, which she understands better." "I vow she would", said the girls, "Well, I say it to his face he did not kiss Kitty once" – this tickled the girls very much, and one of them says to me, "I guess you town's folks dont care for girls much, for by Sammy's account of you, you are mighty shy even of our fresh country girls' – "Why I tell you says Sammy, these town's folks know no more how to behave to girls than a cow does to churn buttermilk. . . ." (July 1789, p. 403)

The slicker again becomes the butt of the joke, and in the process he is convinced that the American farmer is a witty, self-sufficient individual.

The American character exhibited in the "Retailer" paper possesses the same pragmatic, egalitarian quality of which the theorists spoke. His skills are those of practical life – growing grain, keeping stock, raising a moral agrarian family. The Retailer's skills are those of the gentleman – Greek and manners – which, as Rush remarked in regard to education, unfit a man for the circumstances of American democratic life. The American character was best displayed in such a contrast, and its development led to the emergence of native humor as the uniquely American contribution to literary culture.

But the Retailer was alone in giving the American character a literary form. The powerful influence of neoclassical genres caused most American writers of the period to use inappropriate stereotypes rather than to observe the American character and find a place for it in poetry and fiction. The best the *Columbian* can show are stumbling first steps in the direction of a literature which is based on the reality of American life.

5. THE RISING GLORY OF AMERICA

To the writer aware of the socio-political ideals of republicanism the most significant literary theme was the future glory of America.

The Revolution created a zealous faith in progress so optimistic and so idealized that only its sincerity kept it from being ludicrous.[34] American critics and writers based their hopes for a national literature on the distinctive social and political system created by the Revolution. They believed their society was a God-given new chance for mankind to perfect itself; and they naturally expressed its uniqueness in terms of the future.

The American Dream received its most optimistic literary statement during the early national period. The doubts which troubled the 1830's had not yet begun to darken the national imagination. Yet, most scholars who describe the appearance of the Dream in American literature fail to trace it back to its seedtime in the post-Revolutionary decade,[35] in spite of the fact that most of the themes and ideas on which the next century elaborated appeared during those years.

Half a century after the *Columbian* died, William Gilpin described the ideals of American destiny; he wrote in 1846 that the purpose of America was:

to regenerate superannuated nations – ... to stir up the sleep of a hundred centuries – to teach old nations a new civilization – to confirm the destiny of the human race – to carry the career of mankind to its culminating point – to cause a stagnant people to be reborn – to perfect science – to emblazon history with the conquest of peace – to shed a new and resplendent glory upon mankind – to unite the world in one social family – to dissolve the spell of tyranny and exalt charity – to absolve the curse that weighs down humanity, and to shed blessings round the world.[36]

These ideals, which stimulated most of the political oratory and

---

[34] Jensen, *The New Nation*, 87.
[35] For example, Frederic I. Carpenter, *American Literature and the Dream* (New York, 1955), 8, points out that the Declaration of Independence inspired the literature of the American Renaissance, but he does not define the nature of that influence or describe the large body of earlier literature in which the Dream was thematic. R. W. B. Lewis, *The American Adam* is concerned specifically with the literature of the nineteenth century.
[36] *Mission of the North American People, Geographical, Social, and Political* (Philadelphia, 1874), 130. Quoted from Henry Nash Smith, *The Virgin Land*, 40.

patriotic verse of the first half of the nineteenth century, originated in the 1780's and were fully expressed in the *Columbian*. *Columbian* contributors foresaw the day when democratic government would spread freedom to all the enslaved peoples of the world, bringing a new era of simple and natural morals and manners. They also envisioned a growth in American agriculture and commerce so spectacular that some day this nation would be able to supply the world's needs. Enthusiasm over the potential growth of material progress led one essayist to write a dream "Chronicle of the Year 1850" in which he predicted ten wonders that would be accomplished by that date, but his vision in some particulars fell short of the actual growth of the nation.[37] The perfection of science, learning, art, and religion would be concomitant with material progress. In short, America was to be the future salvation of the human race.

When they considered the nature of the American character and government and the limitless availability of fertile lands, most writers doubtlessly agreed with the "Retailer" that in America "every industrious man is likely to be opulent, every virtuous man beloved, and every ingenious man admired" (October 1789, p. 588). Essayists and poets alike foresaw the day when liberty and democratic government would spread to all nations. To them, the United States was "an asylum of liberty, the garden of philanthropy, the theatre of virtue, the temple of science, and the seat of elysium" (June 1788, p. 308) to which men of wisdom would come from throughout the world seeking a pattern of just government. John Swanwick, after describing the pleasures of female company "On a walk in the State House Yard", speculated:

> What various bliss these shaded paths may yield
> To many a nation, whose assembled peers
> May plan their systems on this spacious field
> And in a moment form the weal of years.
>
> (August 1787, p. 610)

[37] For example, his prediction that 150 river boats would be engaged in commerce on the Ohio and Mississippi rivers was greatly surpassed by 1850. On the other hand, his prediction that the delegates from the 30th state would arrive in Washington was only two years off: Wisconsin was admitted in 1848.

Others predicted that the voice of liberty would cross the ocean and produce spontaneous revolutions in other lands. The author of "A Project for Universal Liberty" stated that American liberty had been accomplished "not only to illuminate this continent, and the contiguous islands, but the brightness thereof has dispelled the clouds in the eastern world, and its power has dismounted kings from their thrones, their armies have been put to flight before the standard of liberty" (December 1792, p. 410). "An Ode on the progress of enlightened Freedom" expressed the same idea in verse:

> That voice, which by the western world was heard,
> By the whole world shall shortly be rever'd.
> Despots shall listen to the glorious call;
> Or from their hands their useless scepters fall.

(March 1791, p. 185)

Authors greeted the advent of the French Revolution as concrete evidence of the spread of republican principles. In the September 1791 *Columbian* appeared two poems praising the French Revolution for bringing a new order of *"Equal Rights, Equal Laws"* to Europe. Although the Reign of Terror was later to create a reaction against the excesses of democratic action, at this time the revolution in France seemed to prove the premise of American destiny.

One important effect of the spread of the American political system, writers believed, would be a regeneration of European civilization. The example of the new Adam could redeem the old; the Revolution would "introduce a pleasing change in the knowledge, [and] manners of the people, and abolish the invidious distinction" of European social classes (April 1787, p. 359). The spread of the principles of freedom to other countries would "make as great a reformation in manners and customs, as they have made in government", for "why should the habits of Europe, base in their origin, and debasing in their continuance, become laws to the sons of freedom" (November 1790, p. 317).

A second effect of freedom would be a new flourishing of knowledge. As one writer commented: "Americans, at this aera, enjoying, perhaps, the truest and fullest liberty, in the united states that any political bodies ever did on earth, by their practice, give the best explication to these words, liberal education" (February 1787, p. 264). American universities were hailed as seats of wisdom equal to any in Europe. According to an anonymous poem published in the first issue of the *Columbian*:

> To Albion's shore shall genius cease to roam,
> No more shall wander from its native home; . . .
> From *Harvard's* walls and *Providence*, behold,
> The sons of science flocking to thy fold!
> *New-York* and *Yale* their learned offspring send,
> And *Pennsylvania* greets thee, as her friend.
>
> (pp. 44-45)

Following the advancement of learning, literature and science would flourish. John Quincy Adams, in his Harvard commencement oration (printed in the September 1787 *Columbian*) predicted that "The muses, disgusted with the depravity both of taste and morals, which prevail in Europe, would soon take up their abode in these blissful seats of liberty and peace" (p. 628). The *Columbian* reviewer of David Humphreys' "On the Happiness of America" remarked that "America stands high, . . . in literary reputation: and so great is the spirit which now prevails in the United States, for the promotion of useful learning, and the advancement of science, that, aided by the native genius of our people, we may reasonably expect to arrive at the highest degree of eminence, in these respects" (October 1786, p. 67). In May 1787 the *Columbian* extracted from Joel Barlow's *Vision of Columbus* an apostrophe to American arts and sciences in which Franklin, Humphreys, Trumbull, Dwight, Rittenhouse, Godfrey, West and Copley were advanced as proof of America's greatness. One writer on the prospects of national literature asked: "May we not please ourselves with the expectation of seeing, even in our day, a Helicon and a Parnassus, in some of the sunny hills of the west, – whence streams will issue that will gladden and refresh the fountains of poesy . . ." (October 1786, p. 85).

Even more optimistic were Benjamin Rush's hopes for the future of medicine. Freedom, he reasoned, "by imparting vigor and independence to the mind, is favourable to bold and original thinking on all subjects", and American doctors could perfect the study and practice of medicine, creating "a complete system of medicine" (August 1790, p. 113). Rush felt that not only was the intellectual milieu of his country conducive to scientific discovery, but that its soil might yield new medicines for the treatment of disease:

Who knows but it may be reserved for America to furnish the world, from her productions, with cures for some of those diseases which now elude the power of medicine? Who knows but that, at the foot of the Allegany mountains, there blooms a flower that is the infallible cure for the epilepsy? Perhaps on the Monongahela, or the Patowmac, there may grow a root that may supply, by its tonic powers, the invigorating effects of the savage or military life in the cure of consumption. (March 1789, p. 168)

A third effect of the spread of democracy would be the spiritual regeneration of the Christian church. Writers in the *Columbian* asserted that religious toleration was an established practice in America before it was ever proposed in Europe. A long extract from a review of Provost William Smith's "Sermon ... on the Anniversary of American Independence, 1790" (September 1790) established that Smith's text, Isaiah 52 : 12, "*The Lord hath made bare his holy arm in the eyes of all nations; and all the ends of the earth shall see the Salvation of God*", applied "to the United States, both as it respects a *temporal*, and a *spiritual* salvation" (p. 175). A review of a collection of sermons called "The American Preacher" stated that "because the connection of church and state, which forms a fundamental part of most of the European governments, is a fruitful source of disunion in the Christian church", the separation of church and state and the principles of religious toleration existing in the United States provided "the fairest opportunity that ever was given to mankind to restore union and harmony to the church of Christ" (December 1791, p. 413). This unity being accomplished, mankind would become naturally virtuous. Thus American liberty would bring about the total perfection of the human race, as foreseen in the last lines of a poem on "The Progress of Human Happiness":

Roll on, ye, years, complete the glorious plan,
When man shall venerate his brother man;
When fraudful policy to worth shall bend,
And the whole race in *charity* contend!
When with hosannas heav'n's blest realms shall ring
And truth proclaim, that GOD alone is king!
(November 1791, p. 334)

Few essays or poems on American subjects omitted perorations on
the rising glory, whether or not the rhetorical flourishes were
appropriate to the piece. Often the mere image of America
affected writers as it did Provost William Smith, who concluded
a sermon "Transported at the thought, . . . [and] borne forward
to days of distant renown!" The transportation usually led the
writer to the summit of his rhetorical skill, as it did Smith:

In my expanded view, these *United States* rise, in all their ripened
glory, before me. I look, through, and beyond, every yet peopled
region of the New World, and behold period still heightening upon
period. Where one continuous depth of gloomy wilderness now shuts
out even the beams of day, I see new *states* and *empires*, new seats of
wisdom and *knowledge,* new religious *domes,* spreading around. In
places now untrod by any but savage beasts, or men as savage as they,
I hear the voice of happy labour, and behold towery cities growing
into the skies. (September 1790, p. 177)

Poets, too, described the destiny of the nation. Some saw the
future in terms of immigration and westward expansion. One
poem contrasted the past and present ages, describing the injustice, wars, follies, and superstitions of history from Greece
through Charlemagne, after which time,

Appear Columbus, messenger of peace!
For though thou couldst not bid the tumult cease,
Thy bright example may from horror warn,
Shewing a world to millions yet unborn.
Hither, ye sons of industry repair;
Plough your own soil, and breathe the fresh air.
Sav'd from the woes of war, the wrath of kings,
Here o'er each head her aegis Freedom flings . . .

> Soon shall that age commence, by seers foretold,
> An age of virtue, better far than gold.
> That star, which in Judea shone confess'd,
> Spreads its glad influence o'er the happier west.
>
> (September 1791, p. 193)

To the editors of the *Columbian*, David Humphreys' "On the Happiness of America" epitomized the theme of future glory, and they reprinted it in October 1786, the second issue of the magazine. Humphreys summed up the theme by describing Americans as God's chosen people, given a land of unparalleled wealth and having the duty to spread freedom to all peoples:

> O happy people, ye of whom is giv'n,
> A land enrich'd with sweetest dews of Heav'n!
> Ye, who possess Columbia's virgin prime,
> In harvests blest of ev'ry soil and clime!
> Ye happy mortals, whom propitious fate,
> Reserv'd for actors on a stage so great!
> Sons, worthy sires of venerable name,
> Heirs of their virtue and immortal fame;
> Heirs of their rights, still better understood,
> Declar'd in thunder, and confirm'd in blood!
> Ye chosen race, your happiness I sing,
> With all the joys the cherub peace can bring;
> When your tall fleets shall lift their starry pride,
> And sail triumphant o'er the bill'wy tide.
>
> (p. 68)

Humphreys' vision of American influence spreading reform throughout the world embodied the magazine's ideals and its reason for being. The editors hoped that in literature as in politics they were destined to "See a new aera on this globe begun, / And circling years in brighter orbits run!" (p. 71). Such rhetorical visions of divine destiny, filled with optimism and pride, expressed more clearly than any form of literature that spirit of nationalism which motivated the *Columbian*. Such poems were unashamedly propagandistic. There was no place in the early years of the nation for questioning the truth or desirability of the American Dream. To the American reading public of the late eighteenth century, the vision of the rising glory of America was self-evident, and joyous expressions of that vision perhaps the most satisfactory kind of literary expression.

The *Columbian Magazine* saw the beginning of several national motifs which were expressed during the next century in literature of greater aesthetic interest. The inherent sublimity of the land-scape then escaped the bombastic rhetoric and the need for suitable poetic associations which encumbered it in the *Columbian* and achieved a more appealing expression in Bryant's romantic didacticism and in Emerson's transcendentalism. The Indian continued to develop in his ambivalent nature through Bryant's poetry and the novels of Simms, Cooper, Bird, and numerous lesser imitators. The past provided the subject both for the historical novels of Simms and Cooper and for the psychological probings of Hawthorne, the American character found develop-ment in the sporting papers and western humor, and the ultimate literary expression of manifest destiny was the early Walt Whit-man.

Literary nationalism was, however, only partially successful during the six-and-one-half years in which the *Columbian* was published. American images and themes were bound to conven-tional forms and stereotyped expressions which partially destroyed their effectiveness as literature. Writers had not yet learned to borrow only those images and forms compatible with their national ideals. Although the Augustan drawing room was re-placed by the frontier log cabin, the people in the cabin still spoke with Augustan wit and expressed sophisticated urban ideas.

The peculiar combination of critical theory, literary genre, and American themes in the *Columbian* illustrates two problems which plagued early literary nationalism. First, the editors' critical triad of didacticism, decorum, and correctness contained a self-contradiction. The decorum of subject demanded that authors use American themes and subjects, but correctness of language was based on the literary usage of Augustan England rather than the language of the American people. The resulting literature was false to the reality of American language, even though the linguistic principles which caused the artificiality were accom-panied by a philosophy of realism and decorum which held that literature is good only in proportion to its correspondence to reality.

Secondly, in imitating English genres, authors did not discriminate between conventions compatible with those American ideas they wanted to express and those which undermined them. Stereotyped characters and situations which may have been natural enough to eighteenth-century England were imported to federal America where they were awkward and unbelievable. Writers seemed readier to accept tradition than to attempt to see American life as it really was. Not until romanticism freed the imagination from the authority of literary imitation and linguistic and rhetorical rules could they find a freshness of form and language that was equivalent to their sense of the uniqueness of the American experience.

The *Columbian Magazine* reveals the paradoxes that, although American leaders at the close of the Revolution demanded a national literature and the publishers and editors of the magazine strove to achieve it, the people were too busy building the nation to read or to write it and, although some authors attempted to express American themes, they did so within a destructive framework of English critical thought and genres. American literature in the 1780's and 1790's found itself between two worlds, one dying, the other struggling to be born. The value of the *Columbian Magazine* is that its pages illustrate the early stages of the transition from a colonial to a national literature and illuminate what American writing had been and what it was to become.

INDEX

The following indexes the proper names of persons and periodicals appearing in the text of the book. It does not include the names of scholars and the titles of secondary sources.